NEGOTIATED TERRAINS /

AN INTERVIEW WITH Jeanne Gang

NINA RAPPAPORT How did you establish your independent practice after working for OMA in the Netherlands, and why did you choose Chicago as the place to set up your practice?

JEANNE GANG It was a conscious decision for me to go to Chicago. It is a global city but at the same time a place where I felt I would have the opportunity to design buildings that would actually be built. It was a place to touch down after living abroad and working internationally for several years. I started on my own in 1997 and began teaching as an adjunct faculty member at I.I.T. the same year. Later, I was joined by Mark Schendel, with whom I had worked at OMA, two other architects from Chicago, and several of my students. At OMA I was able to work on two real projects—the Lille Grand Palais and the Bordeaux House—not only competitions. There seemed to be many interesting potentials in the translation of design into construction, so I wanted to continue to build and focus my energies on that. My first project in Chicago, the Starlight Theater at Rock Valley College, was an outdoor community theater, a visible public project that opened the door to getting other public projects. We were lucky to have a great client who was very ambitious, and we were able to elevate his design goals. One of the first things I showed the college was a model of the theater with an operable roof, making the theater functional year-round. Knowing the contractor's capabilities to build large-scale bridges, we argued the idea was achievable—but as it turned out, they didn't need convincing. The dean of the college was a hydraulic engineer and embraced the concept.

NR The theater involved collaborations with engineers and contractors from the outset. How does your built work contribute to an innovative way of working?

JG I enjoy collaborating with team members, especially with the engineers early in the design process. We involve consultants at the start of each project in order to pool our experience on similar building types. When there is good collaboration and a consistent flow of communication, there is a chance for discovery during the process. At I.I.T., in Chicago, I co-taught a studio with engineer Tim MacFarlane, and later we collaborated on the Starlight Theater.

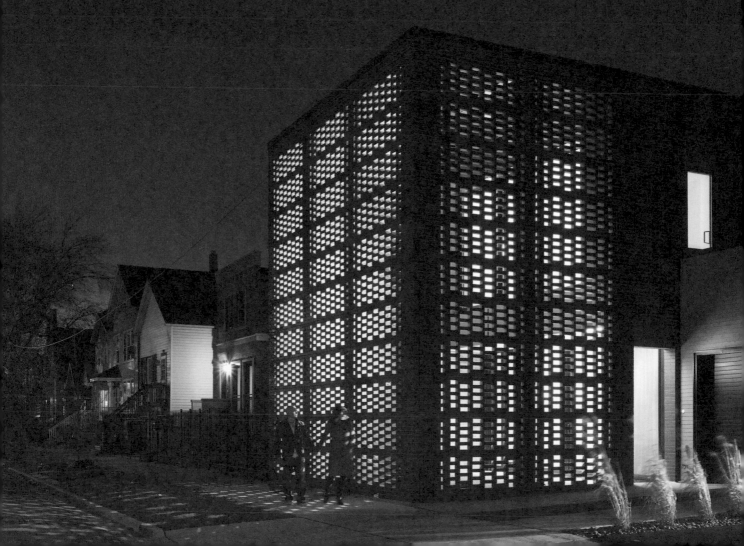

NR What role does structure play in your design process? Does it determine the form, or is it integrated in your designs, or is it an aftereffect?

JG Structure has a lot to do with form for us, but it is one of a number of criteria we work with. Structure is, however, a primary component that is critical to how the building is conceptualized. Many of my interests are connected to structural ideas, such as expressing the thinness of a material or revealing how something is made. Structure is a component; it can solidify your idea or even liberate it. In the *Masonry Variations* installation at the National Building Museum in 2007, for example, the idea was about how the stone could perform in tension. We had to find a balance among materials, form, and the process of making in order to hang a marble curtain in tension from the museum ceiling. It hadn't been done before. The convex shell shape took out lateral loads, while the interlocking puzzle-shaped pieces allowed the curtain to hang in tension. It is a complete integration of structure, form, and craft. A design like this cannot be achieved by the architect alone.

NR Speaking of design, how do different materials inform your making? Do you see craft as a formal way to understand the process of building itself?

JG Our interest is in wanting to take material further, which is why we can't ignore how it is put together in the field, the scale of the material, and the way it gets connected. The Brick Weave House includes a lightweight, lacy brick screen. Before talking to the engineer about the idea, we worked first with masons, who knew the particularities of mortars. Then we talked with the manufacturers of masonry hardware to find ways of customizing ladder trusses and ties to achieve the lateral stability of the wall. The structural engineer wants to use masonry to make the construction stiff, while the mason recognizes the need for movement. Ultimately everyone has to agree, but the point is that different projects emphasize different collaborators at different times in the design sequence. Here, in order to achieve lightness and delicacy with masonry, we really needed to consult with craft workers.

NR Are you trying to create a material effect in conjunction with the signifi-cance of structure to give meaning or justification to the materials of a project?

JG With the screen I was conceptually relating masonry materials with fabric, and I was trying to reveal something new about an ordinary material we take for granted. At the same time I was trying to dematerialize the wall at the lot line. The screen creates a porous layer to the street but maintains some privacy, like a veil.

NR How have you employed tectonics for a building of the non-profit SOS Community Center in Chicago, as opposed to building for a privately funded institution? Are the materials and construction for a non-profit building different?

JG For the SOS Community Center we took a circumstance—that the project would receive donated in-kind materials for construction—and turned it into an essay about concrete and its qualities. There was very little budget, and we were being offered donated material to complete the building. Concrete is a material that looks very different as you change its mix. It also looses its fluid quality when it cures. The idea then was to create a horizontally banded structure comprising differing mixes. Structurally, the different strengths would work together to achieve the cantilever. Visually, the fluid quality would be preserved through the wavy banding in the walls. We worked closely with the tradesmen on techniques for placement and keeping the slump low so that the finish elevation could be varied by up to two feet.

NR How did you incorporate the contributions of the tradesmen and use the constraints of those materials to enhance the project and turn them into some positive form of application that also then becomes research?

JG Rather than refuse the donations to keep our design process "pure," we created a system to organize them so they could be incorporated, which meant infusing the design with flexibility and maintaining a certain objectivity, as if working with variables. Donations such as windows, a revolving door, and carpet lived on a spreadsheet, which we used to track them. SOS shows how unique criteria can influence a design in an interesting way, as opposed to applying a formal idea to a project a priori. Every project has unique challenges, goals, and desires. What we do in our practice is to flush out those unique issues or criteria and intensify them. In the process, new things emerge, and

ideas come forward that solve difficult problems in new ways. We try to do as much fact-finding as we can so that the base of knowledge enables our imagination to make a leap. So instead of starting with a form, we begin with research.

NR If your research is based on multiple aspects of a project—site, context, program, environment, materials—does that overwhelm your project or get in the way?

JG It is so easy now to compile loads of information, but one thing usually rises to the top in terms of importance. For example, for the Ford Calumet Environmental Center we completed research on climate and habitat and learned the environmental and cultural history of the former industrial site. Finding out that 97 million birds die a year in glass collisions struck me as a significant issue that could inform this design because it was essentially a nature center located in a sensitive bird habitat. So we focused on creating a physical manifestation of that issue. A professor at Muhlenberg College, Daniel Klem, had experimented with preventing birds from hitting glass and found that exterior screens performed well. This led to our design of a porch enclosed by a basketlike mesh made from salvaged materials from the region. This woven metal mesh envelops the building, creating a compelling space for people to watch birds while preventing the birds from flying into the glass.

NR What happens to your research-oriented firm as you take on larger-scale developments as well as high-rises?

JG We are interested in the complexity of a project, no matter the scale. We have just completed Aqua, a high-rise in Chicago that has both complexity and scale. The developer wanted a unique building a block north of Millennium Park. The site is adjacent to three levels of infrastructure, an electrical substation that had air rights, and right-of-ways that had to be preserved, so it was difficult. The building is an 82-story residential tower and mixed-use project of about 1.5 million square feet. We addressed the owner's criteria about views, and by intensifying this issue the design emerged. It is exciting to be working on large buildings where the tectonic scale shifts. Instead of working out the details of hardware used for a masonry screen, it's about conceiving a structure that can be built quickly.

Digital design tools allowed the varying slabs to be laid out and built on a three-day-per-floor cycle.

NR How are you able to move your research beyond a specific project toward civic issues and urbanism, which involve the politics of a building—such as the *Baseball in the City* project at the 2004 Venice Biennale?

JG We explore projects that are about the city in order to instigate change. Before the Biennale we had been researching urban areas around baseball stadiums and observed that Chicago has two very different stadiums: one encourages urbanity, and the other rejects it. Through research we thought about a stadium's effect on a city, but we had never designed a stadium until we were asked by *Architectural Record* to reconsider the building type for the Biennale. Our hyper-urban baseball stadium was convincing because we located it above the city's infrastructure, such as existing parking and transportation, rather than isolating it in a vacant parking lot. Our stadium showed how the city could sponsor events yet fold away and disappear when not in use.

NR It seems you are provoking urban design issues in a very pragmatic way. What other urban dilemma's have sparked your interest? Do you ever push an idea beyond the boundaries of what architects and architecture can do?

JG With the stadium, the missing piece was the economic data. I think we could show that supplying single-use parking is actually less profitable for a city than allowing it to be organized more organically. The city surely benefits more from the stadium's food-and-beverage tax than it does on parking spaces that are vacant most of the time. So in this sense the urban issue goes beyond architecture, but it is certainly possible to expand an urban study into these realms.

NR What other projects have allowed you to investigate issues of urban significance?

JG In addition to stadia we have addressed phenomena such as casinos in American cities. We developed a concept for a land-based "eco-casino" in downtown Chicago. What appeals to me are issues that emerge organically but have yet to be addressed through design. Casinos are popping up in

cities outside of Las Vegas, but they are relegated to rivers and parking lots near airports. We asked ourselves if this program type could be reimagined and brought out into the open.

NR How does research help you on unfamiliar projects and programs?

JG As we have begun to work on issues in different contexts and countries our research method has served us well. In India we are working on a part of a much larger master plan in Hyderabad. Research helped us understand the way of life, climate, and particularities of living in that city and allowed us to develop strategies to respond to these criteria, even though the project is literally worlds away.

PREVIOUS PAGE Studio Gang Architects, SOS, Children's Villages Lavezzorio Community Center, Chicago.

ABOVE Studio Gang Architects, Baseball Stadium, *Transcending Type,* installation at the American Pavilion Venice Biennale, 2004.

Assembly as Medium

Even though the success of any building is inextricably linked to the performance of the workers who build it, architecture at times attempts to disassociate itself with its own nasty underbelly: construction. After all, construction is the hardest variable to control and simultaneously the easiest one to blame on others when things don't turn out quite right. It is difficult to hide problems encountered in construction when, at times, compromises and mistakes are transformed into physical monuments. Thus, reducing the variables introduced by physical labor and built construction, as well as finding ways around its inconsistencies, seem like reasonable aims. Recent architectural projects have strained to remove labor from fabrication. Postmodernism's focus on façades is one example—less can go wrong when dealing with this singular element. Prefabrication is continuously revisited as a way to control a design's built results and avoid messy construction. Digital fabrication, luring each architect into becoming his or her own builder, is another way to mitigate reliance on laborers. In the future, fully robotic construction promises a solution. Perhaps the tendency to want to erase labor from the process of building is due to the fear something will be lost in translation from design to construction—from one language to another—so that the architectural intent may be misinterpreted or fall between the cracks because of cultural context, phrasing, or hidden innuendos.

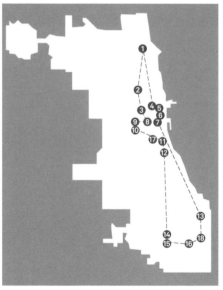

1. Graceland cemetary
2. Finkel & Sons (world leader in die steels)
3. Union row, teamster city
4. Haymarket incident site
5. Lake and franklin wholesaler's buildings
6. Printer's Row
7. Hull House
8. Battle of the viaduct
9. Home of Harold Washington
10. Mexican fine arts museum
11. Former McCormick plant
12. The forum
13. Bessemer Park
14. Philip Randolph Museum
15. Pullman vistor's center
16. Acme Steel Museum and School
17. Stone Gate to the old Chicago Stock Yards
18. Steel workers local 1133 Union Hall and Memorial Day Massacre Memorial

Chicago labor-history trail.

How might this notion be altered if ideas about architecture originated in the material itself rather than in the formal language or design concept? What if the labor-built component of a building was the operation that literally brought an idea to life? Some architects have been testing this notion, with ideas about material and making preceding any kind of formal exploration. This foregrounding of material and making reveals inherent qualities about architecture that are often hidden from view, similar to the way in which a Jackson Pollock painting highlights the materials of paint itself and the physical act of painting. Engaging materials and labor-built construction while simultaneously incorporating automated fabrication technologies are not mutually exclusive.

This Yale advanced studio was organized to explore opportunities in medium, material, and making. The goal was to move into new territory for invention by using physical experimentation in methods of making, stretching analysis beyond but not excluding traditional issues of program, site, and form. How might making's operative words—*pouring, bending, stacking,* or *attaching*—suggest ideas for architecture that could inform site approach, programmatic combinations, or formal interests?

A labor and immigration rally in 2008 demonstrates that labor history continues to evolve as workers contend with the dynamics of global economies, capital, and politics.

The selection of a museum of labor as the subject of the project deepened our historical understanding of work, the work of making, and its relevance to contemporary conditions. At the same time, it revived awareness of the first American labor movements, which seem refreshingly authentic and heroic in contrast to contemporary portrayals of labor-union squabbles. A new look at labor history might, as stated earlier, relieve the architectural profession's intellectual dissidence with the fact that it is primarily laborers and labor—not robots—that continue to build buildings. The studio attempted to reestablish ties between material, builder, and architect in an age when technology offers a potential truce.

Because of its crucial role in shaping early labor organization, Chicago was the focus of the studio's inquiry. Chicago's central continental location, well-connected railroad lines, and abundant resources were important to its explosive growth at the end of the nineteenth century. These characteristics also created opportunities that attracted both factories and job seekers. In fact, the forces

dictions, and diversities that would lead to previously unimagined and potent combinations. The studio was intended to recognize the expanding role museums play as living educational institutions. Central to the studio, however, was the desire to recognize the important contemporary role working-class laborers play in our cities, both domestically and internationally, and to find a way to tend to the identity and growth of this important population.

Jeanne Gang

Images from *On the Job,* a photographic exhibition produced by the Illinois Historical Society in 1976, documenting work. **CLOCKWISE FROM TOP LEFT** casting; iron workers; furniture factory; shoe factory; steel fabrication; television assembly.

BIBLIOGRAPHY

Harold M. Mayer and Richard C. Wade, *Chicago: Growth of a Metropolis,* Chicago and London: The University of Chicago Press, 1969.

Richard O. Boyer and Herbert M. Morais, *Labor's Untold Story,* United Electrical, Radio & Machine Workers of America, Pittsburgh, PA, 1955.

Elliott J. Gorn, *Mother Jones: The Most Dangerous Woman in America,* New York: Hill and Wang, 2001.

Adriaan Beukers and Ed van Hinte, *Lightness. The Inevitable Renaissance of Minimum Energy Structures,* Rotterdam: 010 Publishers, 1999.

David Naguib Pellow, *Garbage Wars: The Struggle for Environmental Justice in Chicago,* Cambridge, MA: The MIT Press, 2002.

Tom Forester (editor), *The Materials Revolution,* Cambridge, MA: The MIT Press, 1998.

Michelle Addington and Daniel Schodek, *Smart Materials and Technologies for the Architecture and Design Professionals,* Elsevier Architectural Press, 2005.

Upton Sinclair, *The Jungle; uncensored,* Tucson, AZ: Sharp Press, 1904.

Erik Larson, *Devil in the White City,* New York: Crown Publishers, 2003.

of industrialization and immigrant labor coalesced in Chicago to create this modern metropolis. When labor and industry found themselves at odds with each other, the city's newfound visibility brought the strife into high relief. The strikes, protests, and formation of labor organizations earned workers a voice and marked Chicago as the center of America's labor movement.

In this context, the studio probed what a studio project for a Labor History Museum could be and what kind of program should be housed there. Many labor-history centers are moments frozen in time, visited to gain a sense of a specific history rather than an evolving one. They tell the story about a place, its people, and their struggle. However, the labor movement is hardly finalized. Its historical representation can be seen as an evolving set of contingencies: a story that changes with the dynamics of economies, capital, and politics. Given the challenges labor faces today—outsourcing of traditional jobs, urban demographic shifts that place workers farther from their workplaces, and ever-changing demands for new skills, for example—the museum project investigated how traditional museum functions might be redefined. To this end, the studio tested programmatic pairings in search of symbiotic relationships, contra-

Labor History Museum

Research on the subject of labor was the first activity of the studio. Students initiated study in five different categories: labor definitions and labor history; the political and cultural aspects of labor; the region's material resources and how they were used for industrial processes; museum precedents and typologies, and, finally, the site's history as the location of labor demonstrations. The second part of this studio assignment was to analyze the discoveries from the research, highlighting and diagraming the most important findings and important aspects. Distilling the work into a visual format made the information clear and accessible to all the participants of the studio. Through this analysis, which provided a social and cultural context for the museum, each participant was able to form a position with regard to the Labor History Museum project.

NIKE AND GLOBAL CONTRACTING

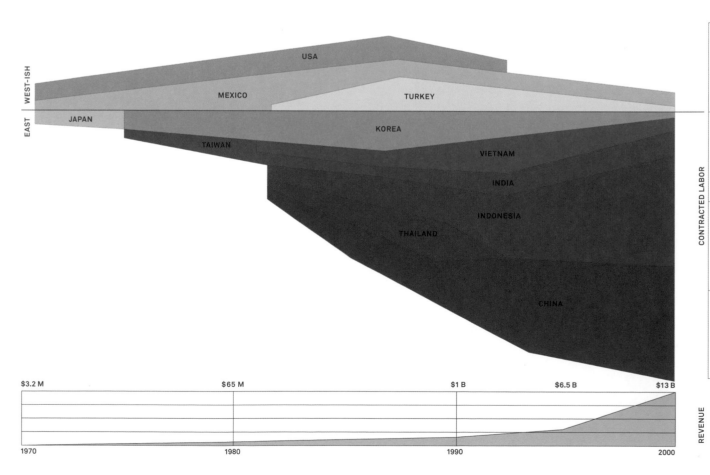

Timeline of Nike Corporation's involvement in global labor contracting (Adam Ganser).

DISTRIBUTION OF U.S. CIVILIAN EMPLOYMENT BY ECONOMIC SECTOR, 1900–2004*

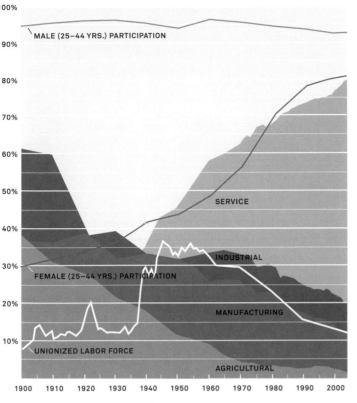

Historical distribution of occupations by economic sector (Fiona Ragheb).
North American Industry Classification System's implementation makes comparable information across time periods difficult.

PUBLIC OPINIONS ABOUT WHAT CONSTITUTES LABOR

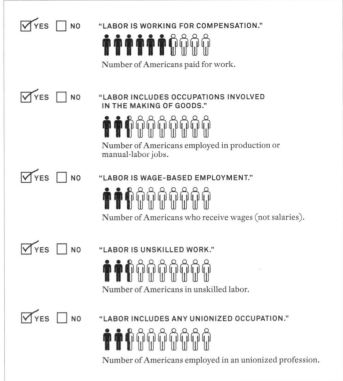

Summary of U.S. Department of Labor Bureau Statistics data of public opinion regarding what constitutes labor (Heather Kilmer).

HISTORICAL DEVELOPMENT OF ANARCHIST THOUGHT

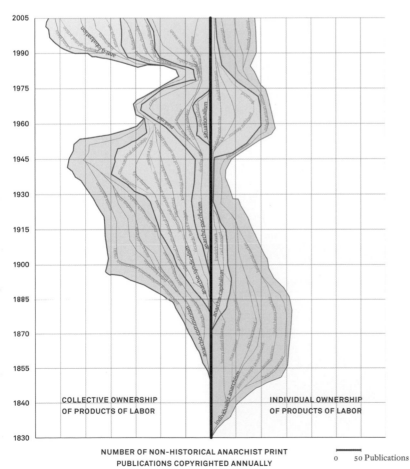

Diagram plotting the historical development of anarchist thought based on ideology around individual or collective ownership of capital (Heather Kilmer).

If playing in the dirt is psychology's contemporary strategy for sound childhood development, playing in concrete is architecture corollary. Materials present the starting point for certain ideas. Their pleasurable tactility or their pressured acquiescence—even their stubborn denial—make them formidable partners in the creative process. Consider the inseparable relationship between idea and material for the glass house, the steel tower, the stone pyramid, or the wooden Japanese temple. In the end, form can only be what materials and methods allow, like a sand castle that resists bulk at its pinnacle lest it lose its tenuous, hand-packed height. Method is the operative action that shapes material, bringing form into being.

design. In doing so, the architect gains a relevant intellectual tool for design. The physical model studies of the studio were intended to posit how an object could reveal its material and how the object itself was made. Consequentially, the larger thesis to be explored was how the design of a museum of labor could use material and construction to give a visible presence and symbolic meaning to workers.

Students prepared physical conceptual models considering materials and making prior to formal investigations. Wax model on left: Marisa Kurtzman; metal model on top right: Adam Ganser; wood-and-Plexiglas model on bottom right: Heather Kilmer.

The studio focused on an approach to architecture that conceptualized "making." In addition to topical research, each participant was asked at this early design phase to examine the properties of materials by executing a concept model employing a physical technique. The concept models were judged on how well they made visible the action that was used to create them and how well the methods employed would transfer to other scales in the building design. This exploration merged designer with "maker," resetting the relationship between form and material. Working with specific material qualities and techniques in creating an object was intended to familiarize the participants with a different way to approach design that begins with material rather than form. Experimentation with material was also used to locate synergies within program and site.

This methodology was especially important for the design of a museum that addresses the concept of work. Building architecture is an act of labor, and architecture maintains a strong tie to physical labor regardless of how technological its design tools become. Architecture can engage and guide the physical actions of its production in new ways by considering materials at the outset of

Les Orear, a 93-year-old labor-history chronicler and director of the Illinois Labor History Society, led our studio visit to important historical labor sites throughout Chicago: the Republic Steel site, the Calumet region of industry, the historic Pullman factory in which Pullman rail cars were assembled, the site of the former stockyards, Teamster City—adjacent to the University of Illinois at Chicago—and, finally, the Martyr's Monument, which is at the site assigned for the studio project. Strikingly vacant, most of the empty large-scale industrial sites revealed the enormous changes that had taken place over the last fifty years in the occupations of Chicagoans.

The specific site for the Labor History Museum, located in the West Loop district, is a place with historical importance to the labor movement. It was precisely at this location where one of the most tragic labor conflicts occurred: the Haymarket Affair of May 4, 1886, was a labor protest that started with optimism and ended in violence, loss of life, and injustice. The protest was organized to decry violence against strikers at the McCormick factory—an event that occured three days earlier—and rally workers to fight for a reduced workweek. They wanted their sixty- to eighty-hour workweek reduced to forty hours, arguing for shorter workdays so some time could be made for rest and leisure.

After a bomb was thrown, a riot ensued and eight police were killed. While no one was proven to have actually thrown the bomb, the subsequent trial of eight alleged anarchists—and execution of four for their political beliefs—is still considered to have been a monumental miscarriage of justice. Because of the ongoing uncomfortable relationship among labor, industry, and law enforcement and their conflicting versions of history, it was not possible to place a significant memorial marker at the location of the Haymarket Affair until more than one hundred years later.

LEFT The studio's site is at the location of the Haymarket Affair of 1886. A marker memorializing the tragedy was difficult for police, labor activists, and industry to agree upon due to conflicting views of the event and its portrayal. RIGHT Located in Chicago's West Loop district, the site currently is bordered by a mix of commercial and residential properties adjacent to train transportation.

In any society, the nature of a memorial evolves with time and the perspectives of those who build them. The Haymarket violence provokes much-contested and divergent memories. The Martyr's Movement was dedicated at Waldheim Cemetery in 1893 to honor the cause of the executed Haymarket labor activists. In 1889, a statue commemorating the policemen who died at the riot was installed on the site; the statue was bombed in 1969, at another time of unrest, and eventually relocated to the city's police academy. Nothing marked the historic significance of the site to the city until it erected a sculpture in 2004 intended to accommodate multiple views of the event. The Haymarket Affair thus provides an important lens through which to view the city today. Placing a Labor History Museum on this site would reaffirm the importance of the working classes who built Chicago and give the city an opportunity to interpret its own difficult past rather than try to erase it.

The studio considered the museum as a living educational institution with multiple programs. In its traditional role, the museum would present artifacts and stories illustrating workers' struggles in historic industries such as meatpacking, steelmaking, farm-equipment manufacture, printing, candy-making, and Pullman rail-car production. The institution also would chronicle (and help visitors interpret) historic labor events and present the struggles that have led to modern work habits. Further, it would shed light on contemporary realities of work around the world and the economics that shape those conditions. Artifacts and historical documents as well as contemporary content would present the issues facing today's service industries in urban centers such as Chicago.

Simultaneously, the museum would provide spaces for the assembly of contemporary workers, forming a community-based worker's club along the lines of the designs for architect Konstantine Melinkov's (1890–1974) Soviet worker clubs and similar organizations in the 1920s. However, in addition to providing entertainment, the building would also include vocational training in labs and classrooms, providing new skills for the changing economy and mechanization of labor. With the project's proposed vocational component, Chicago would be able to shape its own future by retraining its workforce. Lectures, organizing activities, and rallies could be held in the auditorium and classrooms.

The site and its program offered an opportunity to consider how late capitalism will cope with issues of labor and globalization. While the sites of industrial fabrication may migrate to economically advantageous emerging markets, building architecture is inherently local. Local workforces are critical to the operation of hotels, hospitals, transportation, and personal services. The project of a museum of labor history brought forward a need to make work visible by acknowledging the historic importance of the worker's role in shaping society while also making the vital connection between work and architecture in the foregrounding of materials and making in the design process.

The studio work was divided into three organizing themes—Movement, Assembly, Exposure—and described through the lens of each category, which gave the studio coherence.

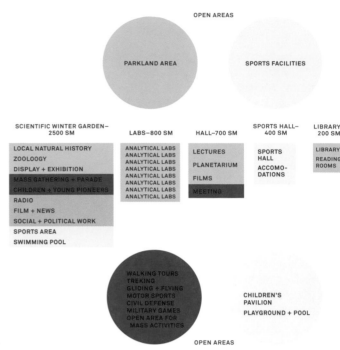

Programmatic and area summary of Ivan Leonidov's worker club prototype (David Nam).

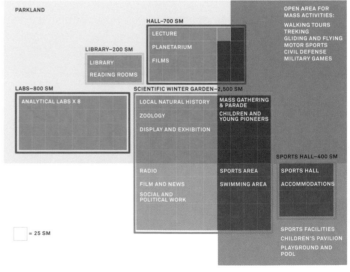

New programmatic events for Ivan Leonidov's worker club prototype (David Nam).

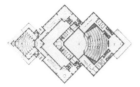

Belogrud, Lenin House
of the People, 1925

Gegello and Krichevsky,
House of Culture, 1925

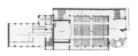

Melinkov, Rusakov Club, 1927

Golosov, Zuev Club, 1927

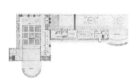
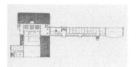

Leonidov, Standard
Workers Club, 1926

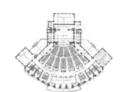

Dmitriev, Palace of Workers, 1926

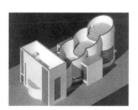

Melinkov, Kauchuk Club, 1928

Melinkov, Zuev Club, 1927

Ginzburg, Standard
Railwaymens Club, 1926

Melinkov, Dulevo Club, 1927

Melinkov, Burevestnik Club, 1928

Golosov and Mitelman,
The Palace of Culture, 1928

1.
Movement

For the visitor to any museum, the unfolding of spaces, experiences, and content is highly choreographed. Evaluating the exhibition sequence, be it chronological or thematic, is an integral part of museum design. Central to the strategy of several student projects was to propose the movement by which visitors to the museum would navigate the building. The idea of the movement in each case was related to the operative movement described by the building's construction. For example, one project organized a spiral movement of visitors that corresponded to the rotating stack of programmatic blocks as well as the stacking of masonry materials that defined them. Another project addressed the need for smooth movement around each wall of the museum and employed the operation of "bending" metal to define the experience. One project re-created energy and flow with the movement of the visitors, "stretching" their path around solid program volumes. Similarly, the skin of the building was stretched across these dissimilar volumes, lending visual tension to the façade.

1.A
David Nam

The Soviet Workers' Clubs of the 1920s, in particular those of Konstantin Melnikov (1890–1974) and Ivan Leonidov (1902–1959), served as a typological model for the Labor History Museum (LHM). Melnikov's projects were organized around a central assembly hall that provided flexibility through the transformation of the relationships between adjacent spaces. This strategy was elaborated through assembly spaces that could be subsumed under one primary space of congregation or broken down into discrete, smaller meeting spaces. Leonidov was critical of the insular nature of prior clubs and sought to expand the club to incorporate the life around it. In his designs he introduced an expanded program (education plus athletics plus expanded gathering spaces) and the use of glass transparency to reduce separation from "surrounding life." Melnikov's spatial organizational strategies and Leonidov's incorporation of all aspects of life within the scope of a building's activities served as points of departure for this Labor History Museum.

Making
The program of the Labor History Museum project consists of three categories: education (vocational school), information dissemination (museum, library, offices), and mass gathering (auditorium, public rally space).

The activity of making was conceptualized as "braiding," in which three separate strands are brought together in form and structure while retaining the autonomy of individual parts. Braiding was employed as the organizational structure of the three programmatic categories of the museum in order to create an ongoing and dynamic relationship among them.

Site
In the past Chicago has tended to build on top of historical sites of ill repute, of which Haymarket Square could be one, but it is not yet covered over. This proposal for the museum opts to retain the ground of the historic site by elevating the auditorium, the largest single space of the program. The lifting of the auditorium enables an outdoor space for public assemblies and rallies, thereby expanding and opening up the space of the museum into the "surrounding life" of the city. A structural vault, formed by bridging the rally staging area and the library, which are at opposite ends of the site, supports the load of the elevated auditorium.

The space of the rally plaza enables visitors to traverse the site, from both Desplanes and Randolph streets. Randolph is the primary artery from the Central Loop to the site. This bias is manifest in the building adjacent to the site; although its primary elevation and service core is on Desplanes, its articulated elevation is on Randolph. This bias reflects the attitudes behind current development in the neighborhood, where restaurants and boutiques have begun to line Randolph.

The auditorium serves as the core of the museum. Its organization permits the classrooms of the vocational school to partake in lectures and activities in the main space while at the same time allowing them to break off into smaller agglomerations or individual classrooms. Viewing spaces on the underside of the elevated auditorium provide a visual connection to the activities below in the rally plaza.

The library serves as the primary entry for the LHM. Its location on the street level enables ease of access to the museum and the research library, thereby promoting an increased public interface.

The vocational school is situated primarily on the south and east sides of the site (facing Randolph). The staging area for the rally plaza serves as the entry to the school. This staging area also serves as a vocational demonstration area. The vocational school is organized vertically. From the entry, students move up to the classrooms and vocational labs, which, at the top, receive good natural light and ventilation. The offices are positioned on the east side of the site, abutting each strand of the program for ease of access.

The museum galleries are organized in a sequence that promotes meandering and a constant awareness of adjacent programs. The gallery sequence is the most braided of the three program categories, interlocking with each in such a way that the museum visitor will always think of the past (historical artifacts) in relation to the present (mass gatherings) and the future (education).

The curatorial concepts include those discussed in the Carl Sandburg Center proposal and in Sigfried Gideon's *Mechanization Takes Command,* including: human movement to mechanization (component operations to standardization/serialization); evolution of the city of Chicago viewed through labor (immigration, rural to urban, population growth, and building technologies); and labor's perspective on how the everyday came to be.

1.A.1 Scheme A, Labor History Museum.

1.A.2 Vault structure study.

1.A.3 Vault structure study.

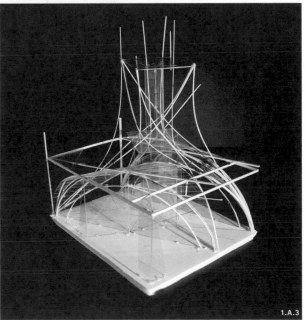

1.A.4 Site plan with public-use flow.

1.A.5–1.A.8 Models of final schemes
from each elevation.

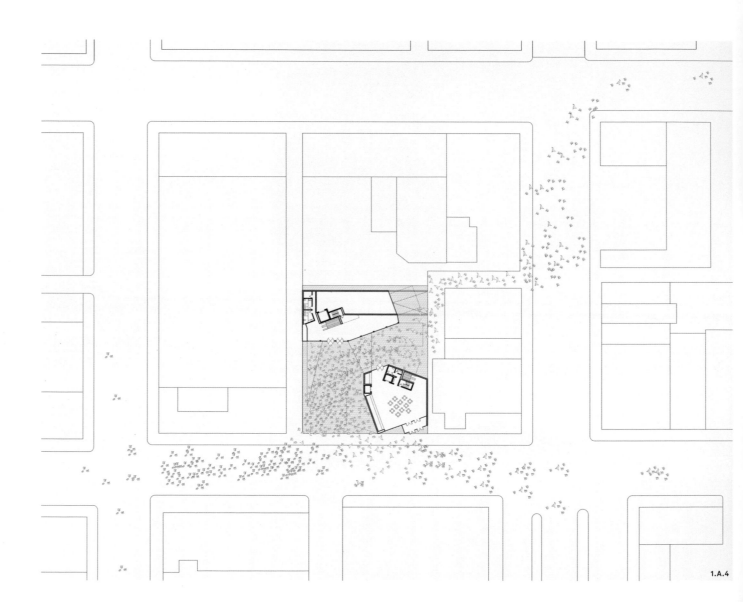

1.A.4

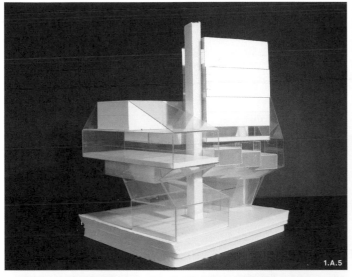

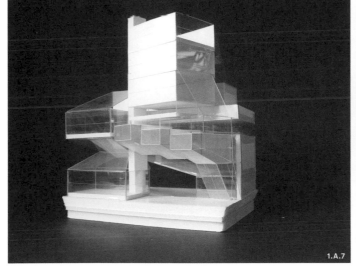

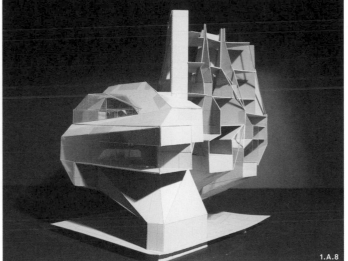

1.A.5

1.A.6

1.A.7

1.A.8

This project explores how Chicago's proposed museum of labor
history can harmoniously contain distinct, unrelated program elements within a single volume, which is a challenge for all museums.

The museum's program prioritizes labor's past, which is preserved
in the galleries, and its present condition, which is addressed
through educational facilities. Because the staff associated with
these program elements have different goals and needs in terms
of their departments and organizational divisions, it was important
to preserve their autonomy yet also encourage mutual awareness
of each activity.

Formally, this discrepancy is expressed as a juxtaposition of
solid spaces, which are used according to specific agendas and set
schedules, and voids—spaces that operate within Chicago's larger
network of cultural attractions and rely more directly on visual
transparency to attract visitors and passersby. In response to the
site's orthogonal, midblock condition within a gridded urban
fabric, the form is a simple cube containing a pinwheel layering of
enclosed educational spaces primarily made of steel and concrete.
This solid pinwheel creates a secondary or residual glassed-in
void that is activated as a continuous gallery surface. The program
elements are thus intertwined yet also function independently.

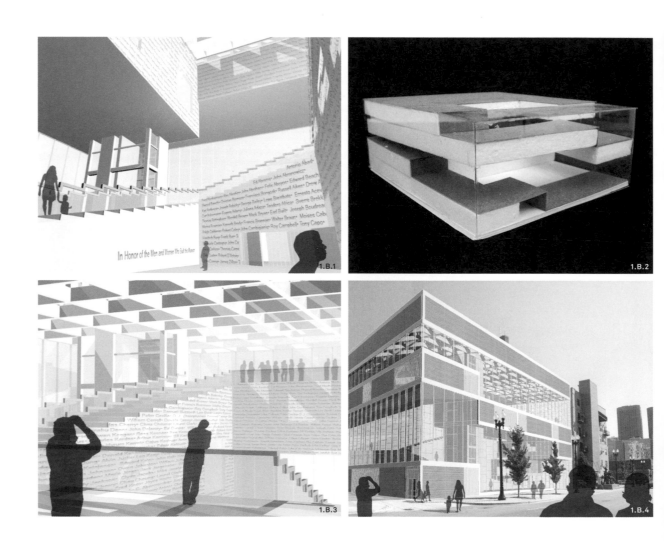

1.B.1

1.B.2

1.B.3

1.B.4

1.B.1 Interior rendering from
the lobby's vantage point.

1.B.2 Process model.

1.B.3 Interior rendering of top floor.

1.B.4 Exterior museum rendering
of entry.

1.B.5 Interior elevation.

1.B.6 Structural model.

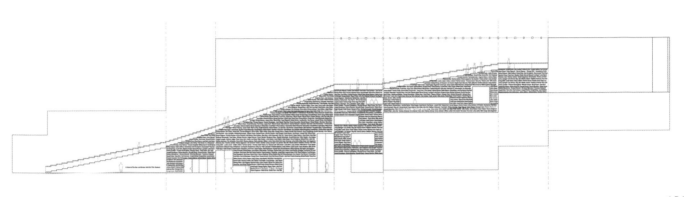

1.B.5

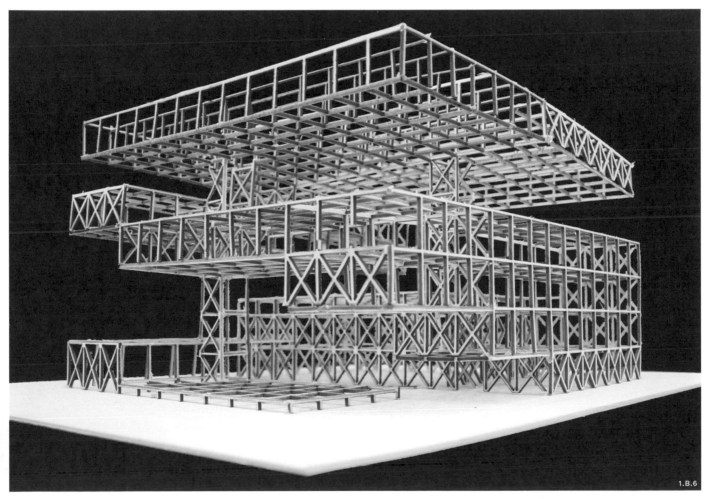

1.B.6

1.B.7 Building-model massing and skin.

1.B.8 Elevation renderings.

1.B.7

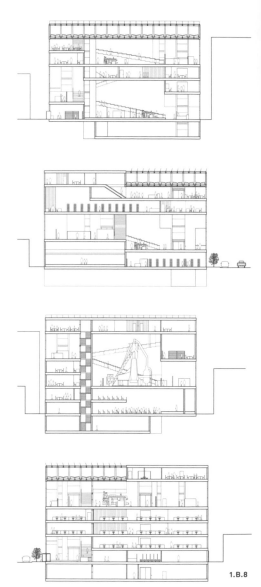

1.B.8

1.C
Abigail Ransmeier

Assembly of all types plays a part in the labor movement. Unemployed masses assemble to wait for work, minorities gather to picket for higher wages, activists march against the World Trade Organization, lines of workers assemble mechanical parts, and robots assemble cars at modern factories. As such, the Labor History Museum can be seen as an assembly line, a continuous flow that displays gallery information while allowing opportunities to assemble, discuss, learn, and listen.

Gallery exhibits are organized in chronological order and follow a system of ramps that circulate through the building from top to bottom. Organized in one line, the gallery is infinitely flexible, accommodating the museum's growth while enabling the disassembly of gallery exhibitions to facilitate larger meetings in gathering areas that overlook the main exhibit/assembly hall.

The museum's private work zones (industrial workshops, vocational training classrooms, and the library) are housed in rectangular volumes inserted in the ramp system. Museum visitors circulate around the volumes, which provide wall space for exhibiting visual art. At three locations visitors can enter "welds," which function as passages that link the public-assembly and gallery areas to the private work zones housed inside the floating rectangular volumes. These passages house digital media screens and computer stations and offer casual meeting areas, which in turn weld, or unite, the two programs: daily vocational programs and the exhibition galleries. This shared media zone displays information about current trends in the labor movement and facilitates conversation among the different museum visitors. The linearly organized museum has the energy of a conveyor belt and references the horizontal assembly of elements in a production line.

The building's structural skin is made of welded metal and glass. The rectangular volumes containing the private work zones are clad in expandable metal mesh embedded in glass and plaster. The composite materials of glass, mesh, and plaster allow for varying degrees of transparency at the level of the museum's interior walls and speak to the larger idea of welding, or uniting, disparate parts.

The museum as a whole foregrounds the assembly process, the materials assembled, the workers, and the work itself.

1.C.1 Structural and circulatory diagrams.

1.C.2 Museum section.

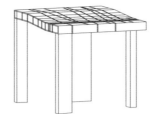

CORES AND TRUSSES

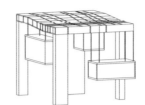

SUSPENDED BOXES

SUSPENDED RAMPS

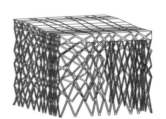

STRUCTURAL SKIN   1.C.1

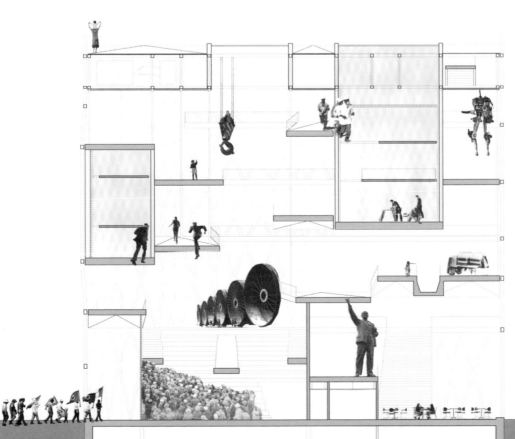

1.C.2

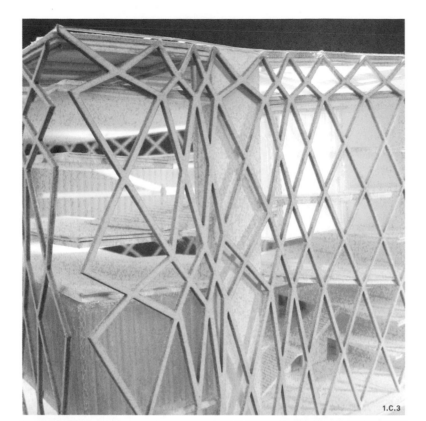

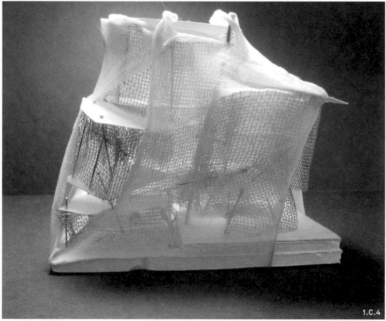

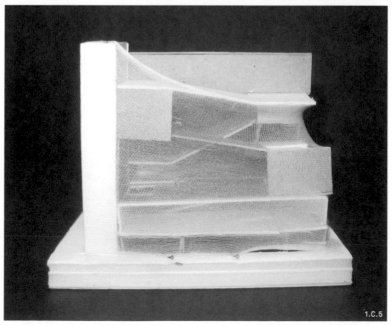

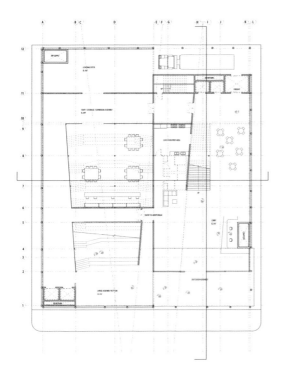

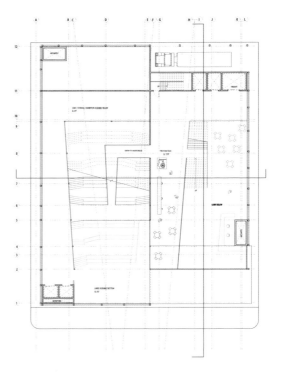

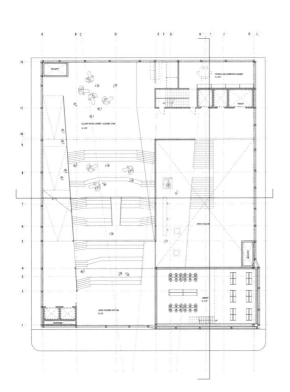

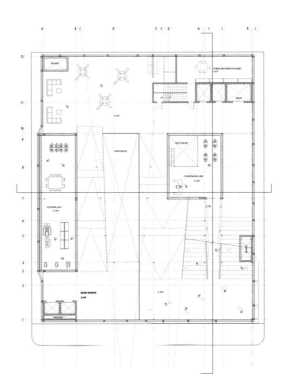

GROUND (1) EL 0'0"
Lobby, café, auditorium, staff,
store and load.

2 EL 12'0"
Pre-function–Library–Auditorium
chute.

3 EL 24'0"
Flex assembly zone.

6 EL 50'0"
Gallery 1850–chute to classrooms.

1.C.6

1.D
Melanie Domino

This project explores the different potentials of the museum wall and contests its conventionally clean, neutral surface. For a museum of labor history, the process of constructing the building becomes part of the story of labor. The act of bending is used to shape the museum walls and create a variety of apertures, displays, and means of circulation, all of which multiply the functions normally associated with a wall—thus coloring the visitors' experience of the exhibition spaces.

A wall can also highlight the theme of work by telling the story of its own construction. Bent steel serves as the formwork, which is affixed to structural concrete walls. The pouring of concrete between the steel formwork exposes the "work" of the building's materials, reversing the conventional wall structure in which reinforcing is located internally. Furthermore, the walls of the galleries along with a structural glass façade eliminate the need for intermittent supports, such as columns.

The program is arranged to encourage interaction among the three main programmatic types—historical, educational, and museum-staff spaces—while simultaneously allowing the museum and training facilities to operate independently of each other. This connectivity creates awareness among the different programmatic elements: The public will have an increased awareness of the conditions facing contemporary laborers, laborers attending classes will gain a sense of pride derived from the recognition of labor, and the exposure to the collections, public, and laborers will enliven the discussion of other approaches to exhibitions and research.

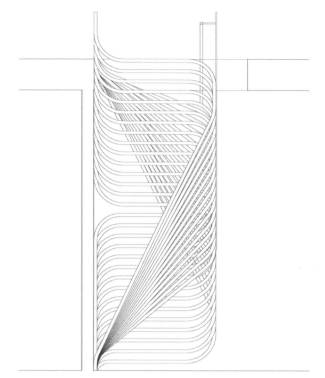

1.D.2

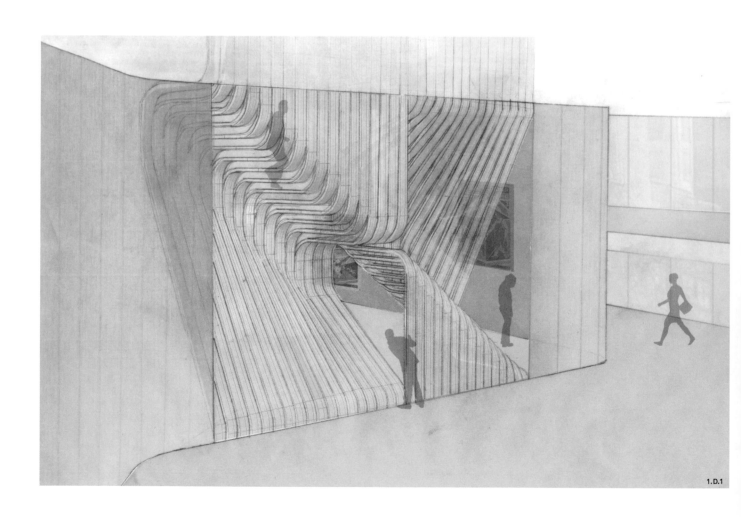

1.D.1

1.D.3

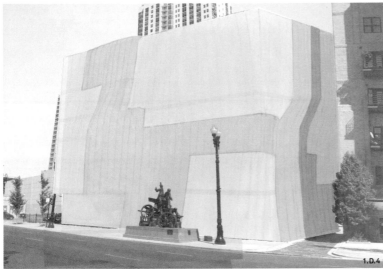

1.D.4

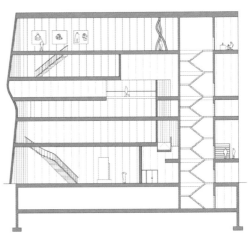

1.D.5

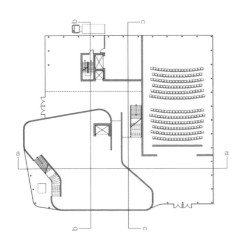

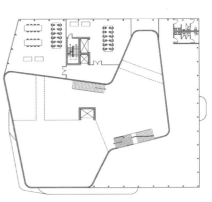

1.D.6

2.
Assembly

Including vocational training and education within a museum program highlighted the different volumetric, usage, and environmental requirements for each. Educational spaces can be used all day and make use of natural ventilation, while archival areas need special protection from atmospheric changes. To provide for the disparate requirements, several students organized the program with methods employed by manufacturing. For example, one project uses a strategy of "packing" for the program with a method gleaned from stacking fruit shipping crates. Building blocks to house educational program were loosely packed on top of each other, with larger exhibition spaces defined between them. Another project employed modular containers to house small galleries and classrooms hanging from a steel structure within a grand machinery hall, which would display large industrial equipment and open onto the street.

2.A
Daniel Chung

In the labor struggle, big business and manufacturers direct a streamlined production through the dissection, evaluation, and specialization of labor into non-skilled, repetitive tasks, which allows for lower costs, the incorporation of robotics, and fewer workers. At the same time, labor unions fight to hold onto worker rights and rally to expand participation of workers with disparate skills and backgrounds.

These activities of dissection, evaluation, and specialization (methods used by big business) and rallying, networking, and reunifying (used by labor unions) are methods that can serve to guide the architectural impulse of the Labor History Museum. While the system used by big business moves toward an increasingly segmented and isolated condition for the laborer, labor unions promote a system that pushes for wider acceptance and recognition of the worker and the workplace and strives to bring together laborers for common goals, benefits, and fair treatment. The dynamic of the two systems is made manifest in the Labor History Museum project.

The spatial translation of the labor struggle provides the basis for two coupled but competing gallery systems. Larger gallery spaces are punctured and nested within smaller conglomerations of spaces; each has a different scale, but all rely on one another for physical support and circulation. The larger galleries offer views that create a complete sense of the assembled spaces and related processes. Each smaller gallery creates an isolated look at individual stages or elements within the larger manufacturing process.

The sectional views between the workshops and galleries are a reminder of the historical roots of the labor movement. The training of workers, the development of skills, the pride of workmanship, and the value of physical work are prominently displayed as the major ground-floor program.

While the galleries have controlled artificial lighting situations with views down and out, the workshops offer transparent spaces with large, open floor plans. Primary circulation areas, administrative services, and mechanical needs are housed in a dense, centralized core from which the galleries and workshops spiral, branch off, and receive support.

The materials selected for the building's cladding allow for the three main programmatic spaces to be visible on the exterior: larger galleries are in precast concrete, smaller galleries are composed of prefabricated steel ISO shipping containers, and the workshops are made of steel-framed, glazed panels. The workshops receive direct shading on their south face from the neighboring six-story office building. On the east and west façades, four-feet-wide permanent catwalks provide high-altitude sun shading and staging areas for worker-crafted vertical sunscreens. The screens are intended to reflect parametric designs that are possible to be fabricated on-site in collaboration with the ongoing building-trades training programs, which are geared toward both construction and deconstruction/recycling methods.

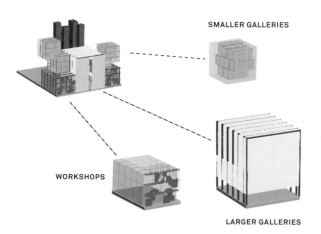

SMALLER GALLERIES

WORKSHOPS

LARGER GALLERIES

2.A.1

2.A.2

2.A.3

2.A.4

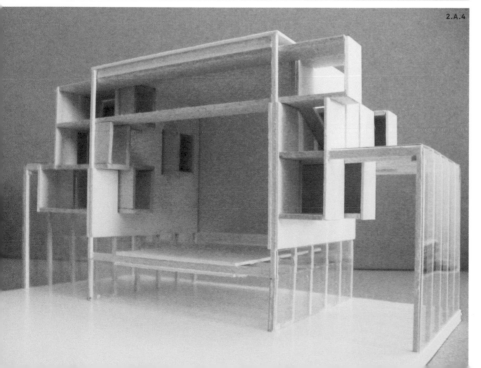

2.A.1 Diagram of programmatic
      volumes.

2.A.2 Building model.

2.A.3 Site model.

2.A.4 Sectional building model.

The Labor History Museum commemorates the history of the Chicago labor movement and provides training for those seeking to improve their position in the labor force. Through investigations of the basic principles of stacking and packing, the design uses close packing to delineate spaces. The design consists of three strategies: separate all programmatic functions into one of two categories, education or exhibition; develop a building block flexible enough to house all the educational programs; stack the education blocks and then separate the stack to create interstitial voids that house the exhibition spaces.

The blocks are clad in masonry to reinforce theme of manual labor as well as to give the educational functions a symbolic weight. The voids between the blocks become a transparent mortar that also gives the building a lighter appearance and draws more attention to the separated blocks. The building foregrounds an auditorium and central rallying space.

2.B.1

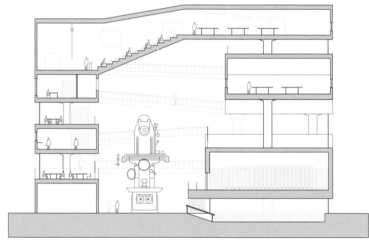

2.B.2

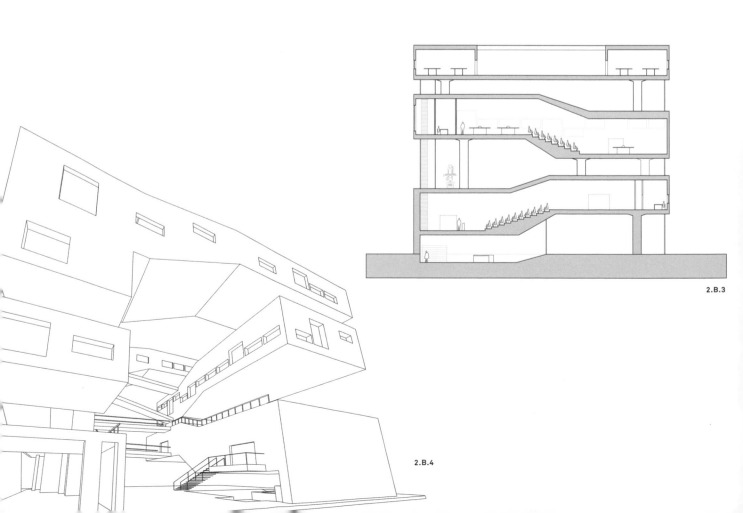

2.B.3

2.B.4

2.B.1 Stacking process diagram.

2.B.2 Museum section.

2.B.3 Museum section.

2.B.4 Exterior perspective.

2.B.5 Metal study model of stacked volumes.

2.B.6 Labor History Museum model.

2.B.7 Axonometric of building volume.

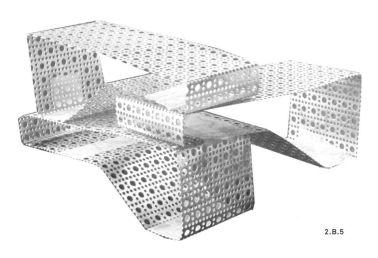

2.B.5

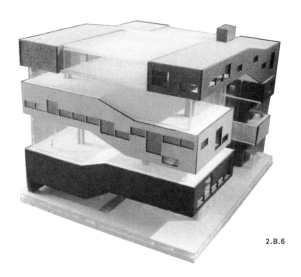

2.B.6

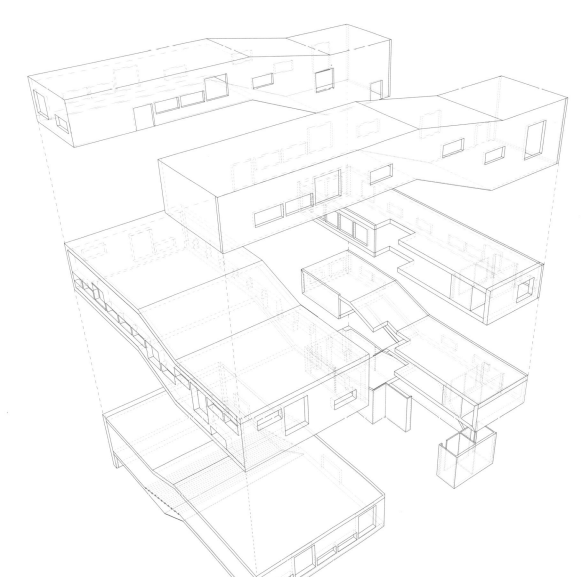

2.B.7

The programs, classrooms and labs, galleries, and administrative spaces are the building blocks of the design. Each program is "slotted" and interlocked with the others, establishing interdependence and connection. The gallery houses the artifacts of the history of labor and provides a context for labor's importance. The education labs offer training to ensure the vitality of labor's role within the workforce.

The interlocking of the labs and galleries emphasizes the pace of a global market and workforce and the need to develop skills that allow for flexibility in light of the market's changing needs. Materially and spatially, the education and history zones engage in the same dialogue and are transparent to one another, while the administrative spaces disappear into the background.

2.C.1 Site model.

2.C.2 Interior perspective of museum lobby.

2.C.3 Museum study model.

2.C.4 Model of interior museum lobby.

2.C.5 View of Chicago skyline from museum.

2.C.1

2.C.2

2.C.3

2.C.4

2.C.5

3.
Exposure

Industrial places have typically been located on the periphery of the city, close to resources such as land and water or housed in loft districts near the urban centers. This marginalization has made the workplace difficult to see and understand. In addition to its historically hidden locale, labor is underrepresented or represented in a conflicting manner, impairing a contemporary collective perception of work and workers. Sensitivity to this invisible condition moved several projects toward highlighting aspects of program usually kept at the back. One project worked with typology to blur the distinction between a warehouse as a place of work and a museum as a place of display. Several plans exhibited typically back-of-program areas—for example, loading— at the front of the building, highlighting the actual work of unloading to museum visitors. These projects tended to also reveal aspects of construction and materiality not usually seen. One employed weathering steel, for example, to reveal the passage of time and related this material choice to a heightened awareness of time, as well as the integrity of work as defying time.

3.A
Heather Kilmer

Time has always played a defining role in labor. Laborers clock in and clock out to mark the beginning and termination of each workday. Days "on" and "off the clock" are predetermined and systematically documented. Labor activists have long fought to maintain a worker's right to time away from work. The polarizing Haymarket Affair was a causative factor in the passing of labor laws related to the amount of time laborers spent at work weekly. Prior to this pivotal protest, workers were laboring "on the clock" twelve hours a day, six days a week. Regardless of class or type of work, the weekend benefits all Americans. The impetus for this proposal was to show how a museum devoted to labor can accentuate the experience and appreciation of time and its role in labor as well as in architecture.

Program
Chicago's Labor History Museum is a 75,000-square-foot semi-public building that contains spaces for historical artifacts as well as for education, training, and cultural activities. Thus, the building must serve as both a museum and a living education facility. The aim of the historical program is to tell the story of labor history, while the aim of the "living" program is to provide vocational training and cultural activism. Despite the different spatial and functional needs of these program types, a visual connection between the living and historical programs is made possible through a central void and the interspersing the program types. Organization of the building's program interlocks the living and historical sections while retaining separate circulation systems. Form, space, and view angles tell a narrative that connects labor history to the museum's present mission of vocational education and cultural activism. Past, present, and future are organized spatially and interconnected programmatically, regardless of a strict chronology.

The intrinsic life of a building is one of change and evolution. If left alone, a building experiences time through the process of material transformation and weathering; however, the architectural preoccupation with newness conceals the aging of buildings and their materials and thus history and time. Newness is reinforced by ongoing maintenance and the modular replacement of aging materials to increase the building's longevity and market worth. In order to underscore the experience and appreciation of time, this project questions conventional notions of newness, maintenance, and material maturation.

Weathering, or material maturation, is embraced in this project as an inevitable occurrence in architecture and as its connective link to time. This condition is made visible in the project's use of material assemblies to line the exterior and central void, which are allowed to weather naturally. These *in situ* concrete exterior walls are constructed with permanent perforated-steel formwork. Rather than removing the formwork after the concrete cures, the formwork remains intact and affixed to the concrete panel to reveal the method by which it was constructed. The unsealed steel is allowed to naturally corrode and stain both the adjacent concrete and the glass. Since the steel is not a structural element, it also is allowed to naturally decompose. Traces of time and material maturation appear on the more resilient materials in the form of discoloration and the perforations created during construction. Time in architecture is accentuated rather than obliterated. The labor museum is constructed with an understanding of its relationship to time and its ability to change and mature.

3.A.1 Programmatic organization: intertwining "living" and historical museum programs.

3.A.2 Massing model study showing how two programmatic volumes interconnect.

3.A.3 Interior model of building circulation and materiality.

3.A.4 Site plans showing entry installation and historical museum program.

3.A.5 Fourth-floor plan showing workers club and social space.

3.A.6 Eighth-floor plan showing working/living program.

PROGRAMATIC ORGANIZATION

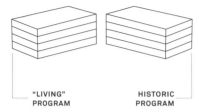

"LIVING" PROGRAM

HISTORIC PROGRAM

TWO PROGRAM TYPES STACKED AND ALTERNATED

3.A.1

VOID INTRODUCED WHERE PROGRAM TYPES OVERLAP

3.A.2

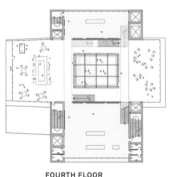

3.A.3

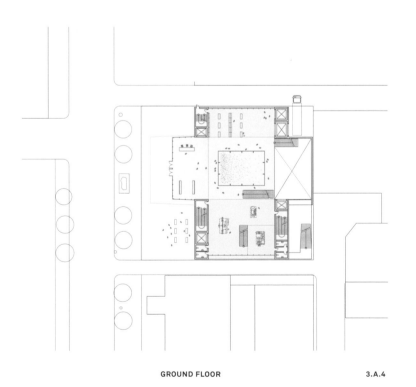

GROUND FLOOR   3.A.4

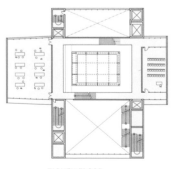

FOURTH FLOOR   3.A.5

EIGHTH FLOOR   3.A.6

PROGRAMMATIC DISTRIBUTION

LIVING EDUCATIONAL & ADVOCACY PROGRAM

SHARED SOCIAL PROGRAM

HISTORIC PROGRAM & MUSEUM EXHIBITIONS

3.A.7 Labor History Museum
exterior rendering.

3.A.8 West-facing section through
central and central void.

3.A.7

3.A.8

3.B
Joyce Chang

The portrayal of the labor unions as villains, rioters, or even police killers in the Haymarket Affair demonstrates an act of deception imposed by mainstream media and the tyranny of capitalism. The story of Haymarket, told from labor's perspective, is a struggle against exploitation and authority, a view less likely to be acknowledged.

Thus, the act of twisting—as a construction method and as a narrative strategy—was chosen at the beginning of the design project in an effort to reveal the untold history of labor struggle. The design of a Labor History Museum for Chicago inverts the relationship between the hidden aspect of work and its public display. The programmatic arrangement of the museum foregrounds back-of-the-house activities—for example, loading and receiving goods in the workrooms and storage areas—and displays them as performances. Structurally and conceptually, these programmatic elements become the backbone that connects together all the public functions.

One of the precedents for this project was the Brooklyn Navy Yards, where a giant gantry crane is employed in the interior of the main building to drop heavy machinery and goods onto balconies. Loading and receiving, in this case, become the central performance in the space, thus thematizes the act of work in the movement of the crane.

The act of twisting also served as a guide in the development of the details. A "twist-tie" connects two objects at a 90-degree angle. Using this action as a physical detail principle to continue the idea of twisting, other variations were created that allow the objects to connect at a third axis. In their size and scale, when incorporated into the façade/stairwell, the connections dramatize the physical connection that celebrates the act of twisting and motion in the act of labor.

3.B.1 Model of museum.

3.B.2 Model of interior staircase.

3.B.3 Museum façade detail.

3.B.4 "Twisting" connection detail.

3.B.5 Multiples of "twisting" connection detail.

3.B.6 "Twisting" detail translated to another metal.

3.B.1

3.B.2

3.B.3

3.B.4

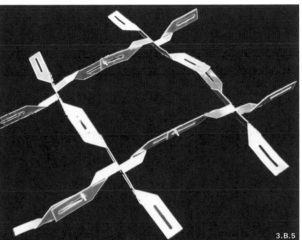

3.B.5

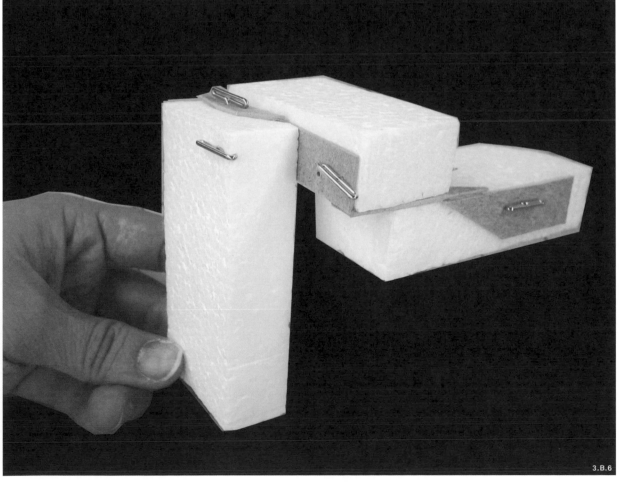

3.B.6

A program for a museum of labor history poses the challenge of how the temporally and spatially defined act of labor can be made manifest in the atemporal realm of architecture. Today the act of labor is translated into an act of education or entertainment, production is translated into consumption, and the mutable is translated into the fixed and unchanging. This issue became the driving force behind the conceptual development of the Labor History Museum, which includes vocational training facilities.

Among the types of work the museum sponsors are those of the museum employees, patrons, building systems, and the content itself. A museum of labor history can highlight the performance of this work and serve as an index of human habitation. In order to reveal these inner workings, the conventional relationship between front-of-the-house and back-of-the-house activities had to be challenged and reconceptualized. The project site–a midblock lot on North Desplaines Street that was the site of the 1886 Haymarket Affair in support of the eight-hour workday–provides an initial cue. Although a midblock site, none of the surrounding buildings front onto Desplaines Street; instead, the site is defined by alleys, neighboring loading docks, surface parking lots, and the side and rear elevations of adjacent structures. This suggests a strategy in which the "working" elements of the program are reoriented in relation to the nominal street frontage.

A conventional program analysis would yield results in which operations are hidden from view and the public is presented with a representation of the image and history of labor. This traditional typological analysis would simply group like elements together and confirm that different departments share some programmatic elements. A performative analysis more significantly examines how components *behave* and reveals affinities between very disparate constituents–for example, both visitors and exhibition artifacts are received by the museum. This approach also demonstrates the way in which the same entity behaves differently in changing contexts–for example, an artifact is considered as storage when in the warehouse, but as an exhibition when on view in galleries.

In challenging the divide between front-of-the-house and back-of-the-house activities, the divide itself became the site for exploration and evolved into a thickened zone housing artifacts from the museum's collection. Simultaneously storage and display, the zone, or wall, migrates vertically through the building from the lower-level loading dock to the roof garden. As this zone moves through programmatic areas, it sponsors varying needs including the coat check (dress or uniform being one of the most visible markers of employment and economic status), the auditorium projection booth (where the projectionist becomes part of the labor exhibition), and museum-store display (commerce being the product of labor). In transgressing the threshold zone/wall, visitors move fluidly from front to back and vice versa, and in the fleeting moment they occupy the threshold space they become part of the display viewed by other patrons and employees. The program is organized into four alternating bands as one moves through the site: a loading zone over which visitors must pass to gain entrance, followed by a program band, a second loading zone comprising storage and a display zone serviced by a freight elevator and gantry, and a final program band. This interweaving of performance and representation, or labor and exhibition, ensures visitors are never isolated from the operational labor at the heart of the institution.

From the exterior, the markings of labor are clearly visible. The loading dock is oriented along the front façade of the museum, thus relating it to the immediate urban context and highlighting the daily operations of the institution. The visitor entry is created by bridging the loading dock, so that both forms of receiving are aligned sectionally. The vocational labs are placed prominently along the entry façade, and their large, glazed expanses are fritted with images of labor, serving as both representation (signaling what takes place inside) and performance (screening rays from the setting sun). At the top level, a roof garden maximizes environmental performance while also taking advantage of benefits from the city's green-roof program.

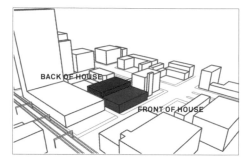

CONVENTIONAL RELATIONSHIP TO STREET

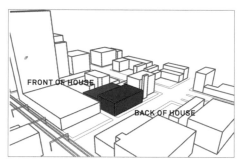

INVERTED RELATIONSHIP TO STREET

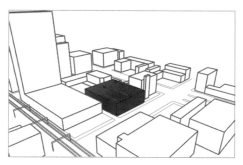

THRESHOLD BETWEEN OPERATIONS   3.C.1

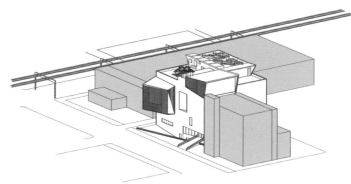

3.C.2

3.C.1 Process diagram illustrating conventional back-of-the-house and front-of-the-house activities in relationship to the museum entry, which is an inversion of the relationship while remaining a "threshold" zone occupying the space in-between.

3.C.2 Diagram of "green" and programmatic elements.

3.C.3 Entry-level plan.

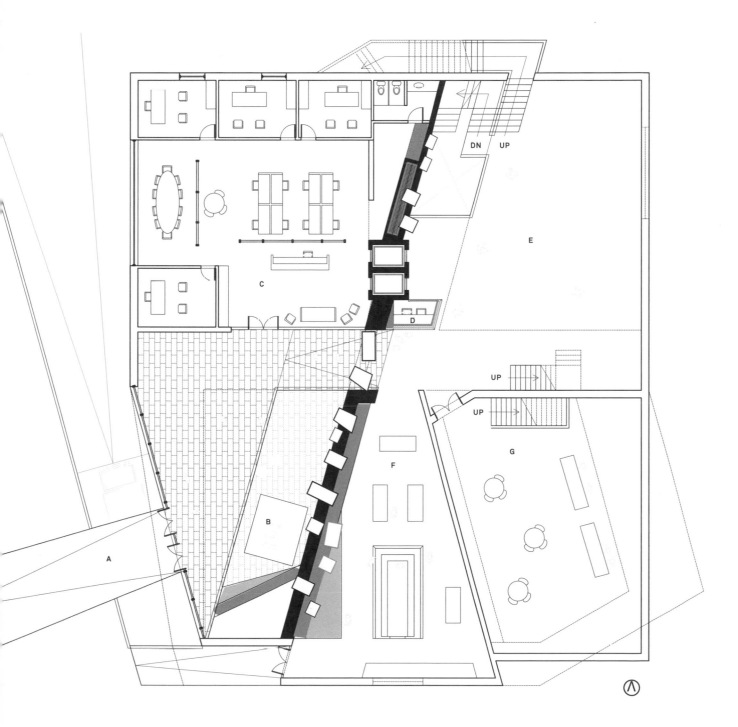

ENTRY-LEVEL PLAN:

A. ENTRY
B. FREIGHT ELEVATOR LIFT
C. STAFF OFFICES
D. ADMISSION
E. LOBBY
F. MUSEUM STORE
G. CAFÉ

3.C.3

Sunil Bald
INSTITUTION DISSOLUTION

LEFT Studio SUMO, Josai School of Management, raised inner courtyard looking to glass bridge, Japan, 2007.

BELOW Studio SUMO, Project Rowhouse, view of shotgun path, installation, Houston, Texas, 2003.

AN INTERVIEW WITH Sunil Bald

NINA RAPPAPORT How have you jumped from small-scale projects in New York to your recent large-scale business-school project, Josai University, which was just completed in Japan? Where have you found your architectural skills being expanded beyond architecture? It is interesting that quite a few other New York architects, such as Jim Polshek and Steven Holl, did their first major buildings in Japan in the 1970s and 1980s.

SUNIL BALD While the shift in scale and place definitely held challenges for my partner Yolande Daniels and myself, we did have experience from which to draw. On the one hand, we were already quite familiar with the client, having taught at Josai, each summer, since 2000. Following a lecture at the school about our work during our third summer semester, we were asked to develop ideas for two tiny sites near one of the university's campuses—a project that was never realized. Eventually, the university also asked us to look at a much larger site for a new business school at another campus, but by then we were quite familiar with them as clients and already had an understanding of the culture of the university. Furthermore, I had worked for Antoine Predock years before on comparable projects, so scale wasn't as daunting as the issue of how something gets built in Japan, as well as learning ways of interacting with people from a different building-and-design culture. The culture of practice in Japan was something completely new but in the end extraordinarily rich and rewarding.

NR What was your approach to the design of this project once the program was figured out? Did they give you free rein?

SB Not exactly, although in our limited experience it does seem the architect in Japan is given more responsibility in shaping program rather than just accommodating it. We did play a large part in shaping the program, but we interacted closely with a building committee consisting of the chancellor and the school's deans. They entrusted us with design decisions to a great extent because there were clear programmatic protocols to which one needed to adhere. Still, we did begin by operating under certain assumptions. We started with a very generic collection of volumes: offices, classrooms, two auditoria, and a maximum 10-meter structural span for a concrete column/slab system. Without much to go on in forming interior programmatic relations, we asked what kind of architectural object would organize the exterior part of this disorganized edge of the campus. As a

result, probably the most interesting spatial experience of the building is staying outside of it and slipping through and inhabiting the exterior spaces it organizes. Sectionally, the first-floor slab lifts up to allow this slippage. The public spaces on the first two floors conform to the landscape and mediate between the different elevation shifts of the site, connecting the building to the hillside. This element also forms the base of the three-story classroom bar, which is a single loaded corridor; its 300-foot length winds back on itself in a J-shape: a three-story glass-bridge hairpin. Though we didn't set out to make a J-shape, the school was happy with it, so we went with this symbolic flow.

NR How have you learned from these operative insertions in terms of them being instrumental in the design of this project? Your earlier projects, such as Flip-Flop and the FemmePissoire, related to sculpture detail and objects in a space. Does this project relate to the same issues, just with more square meters?

SB That previous work did deal with highly defined programmatic instrumentality, but in this institutional setting we were much less directive, making opportunities rather than mechanisms for activities. Josai is a large building, so we had to look to the interstices for these moments—a small kink that might create the slightest widening, and in the smallest space there would be an intensity of occupation—making the cracks in our own design. The school's faculty wanted spaces evoking hotel lounges in which perhaps work gets done informally rather than in a conservative boardroom-like setting. In these spaces the insertions were much closer in scale and concern to our previous design interests. Further, we designed the furniture and had more control within the modest budget.

NR What elements have transformed your projects in a larger way, such as recoding a norm in an unexpected solution or creating an irony in a project, as in your *Shotgun House* installation or the Mini-Max prefab home? How is the reworking of a program or an idea to express a project more important than how they are normally seen to transform beyond the expected, everyday situation?

SB We are interested in how everyday situations, when overly interrogated, might have something of a greater importance you normally wouldn't

ascribe to them. Both the *Shotgun House* and the mobile home are examples of the American vernacular, but this country has always been able to conflate the prosaic with something extraordinary. The *Shotgun* installation at Project Rowhouse helped us understand the relationship of shotgun morphology, environmental performance, and domestic structure. In proposing Mitan, twenty-two units of affordable housing in the Little Haiti neighborhood of Miami, we were able to reconfigure the house as a building block that would maintain the performance and program of the traditional Creole-house precedent but within the framework of an apartment building. In this case, the demands of the unit—along with some crazy zoning and parking regulations—determined the morphology of the building.

With Mini-Max, we began with simple observations of the domestic aspirations symbolized by minivans and the accelerated obsolescence cycles of digital commodities such as iPods—not unlike issues explored by the Smithsons' Appliance House from the 1950s. While the manufactured house depends on an economy of scale to be feasible, most buyers want to think of their house as permanent, not as a consumer item with a finite life. This led us to look at basic domestic programs to see if a house could not only absorb the economic system that allows it to exist but also question its permanence. Our spaces are increasingly defined by components rather than by walls, and they are predicated on one's interaction with those components. The interchangeable components led us to make a series of movable dashboards as walls, so that the room could change according to the component you want to "turn on." These components are linked by bellows, like those used for New York public buses.

NR While Sir Richard Rogers's early work, the Smithsons's work, and the plug-in houses are rather high-tech, your Mini-Max house is more about found technologies than new or futuristic ones. There is an interesting correlation between Flip-Flop and the components in Mini-Max. How do you see the relationship of the body to the space in Mini-Max as different from that of Flip-Flop, which is really more of an art form? Is one more generic and the other more specific to your space?

SB Flip-Flop had a more direct relationship to the body, wherein the body had to conform to these manipulated found objects, and they in turn had to conform to you. Mini-Max is a bit more about technologically outfitting

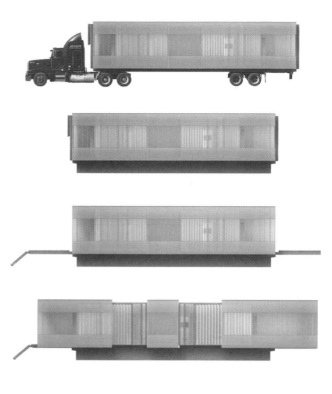

LEFT Studio SUMO, Museum of Contemporary Diasporan Arts, Brooklyn, 2006.

BELOW Studio SUMO, Mini-Max, site view, aerial view and deployment sequence.

and spatially altering your environment rather than being high-tech, as you say. Flip-Flop was based on an "off the sidewalk" economy; Mini-Max is very off the shelf, or "off the Web," in how it is made and in what it contains. But the process of making and acquiring these "shelf" items still has to be coordinated and developed for it to be feasible.

Another recent long and narrow residential project, the Leaney Duplex in New York, incorporated some of these ideas into a more stripped-down commissioned project in which the rooms were removed and the components were dependent completely on the walls and objectified as moments in the space—though the open shower is definitely a more luxe version of the wet space in Flip-Flop.

NR Do you consider similar issues with your art-gallery spaces, both of which are renovations: one for the Museum of African Art's (MAA) temporary space in Long Island City, and the other for Brooklyn's Museum of Contemporary African Diasporan Arts (MoCADA), which presents white-gallery/loft spaces without the orientation of objects. Is the white-box space something you have consciously considered?

SB It has been interesting to take on the question of the white-box gallery for these two clients. We are not fighting it, but we are struggling with it. The MAA project was a low-budget renovation, eighteen dollars a square foot, so they couldn't really afford new walls. We used construction fencing and other economical materials for finish surfaces in the lobby and gift shop, as well as a system of cables for hanging fiberglass paper in the gallery space. It is important to note that, in a space for African art, white is not necessarily a "neutral" color but one associated with concepts as extreme as death in some of these cultures. African art questions our assumptions about neutrality, and as an institution the MAA has historically reconceptualized notions of display. Our orientation was really more focused on how to address and project the temporality and transience of this institutional space. MoCADA is a fledgling organization in Bedford-Stuyvesant, but it is moving into a new space in the new BAM Cultural District. It has been an art space for its community and now is growing into a space for the art community, making it an architectural challenge to balance these two institutional aspirations. The latter is predicated on the complexities and messiness of identity, the former on the neutrality of a space for art. Rather than identifing an aesthetic specific to the African diaspora, we focused on the notion of the diapsora itself: how the spatial mapping of the (usually forced) migration and scattering of a continent's people might be communicative while also having its own spatial or tectonic integrity in a map that we designed for the lobby space.

We are confronting the white-space dilemma in yet another context, this time in Japan for the Mizuta Museum. While still in the design-development phase, there is no white space—just one black box and one box with filtered natural light contained within the volume of the museum. The black box will house a valuable collection of woodcuts in a space in which the space itself is meant to completely disappear and the colors of the prints pop forward. The naturally lighted gallery is meant to show work from the community—not precious, but important and always changing. It is interesting that the middle ground of this binary, the neutral white space, does not exist in this particular scenario.

NR How do you consider the narrative of architecture in regard to your research on Brazil as well as the historical work on politics and power you incorporated into the Yale studio? If narrative makes the work more political, realism has more potency in regard to sociopolitical and economic issues. So would you say narrative in architecture is the space assisting in the process of telling the story indirectly?

SB In my Brazil research I have looked at narrative as the history that is contemporaneous with the architectural object; it is written simultaneously as the architecture is made. I have been looking back at the mythologies—including Brasília's—that were written to frame the architecture culturally and politically. Instead of architecture shaping identity, it examines the identity of architecture. Of course, buildings and narratives—having very different types of presence in our physical and psychological worlds—can and do become dislodged from each other or establish new affiliations.

NR Are you conscious of making a narrative in your own work, or do your projects tell a story about another time and place?

SB Narrative is sometimes in our architecture, but it is not direct and not something with which we feel entirely comfortable. In the installation at

LEFT TOP Studio SUMO, Josai School of Management, media room and classroom circulation, Japan, 2007.

LEFT BOTTOM Studio SUMO, Josai School of Management, exterior facade, Japan, 2007.

ABOVE Studio SUMO, Mitan Affordable Housing, north elevation (shotgun units), south elevation (manor units), court elevation, renderings, Miami, Florida, 2007.

Project Rowhouse in Houston's Third Ward, we employed narrative to show there was something there that hadn't been there before, to acknowledge an erasure. The Shotgun House has been traced back to West African dwellings as a vernacular that became slave dwellings or houses for the poor over here. So how do we work with it so the house tells its own story? It is also an architectural history that has been marginalized, so the only way we could look at it was through narrative. We found amazing stories about the domestic lives of slaves and wrote them on the surfaces, giving the words a material quality through surface and shadow to architecturalize the narrative, rather than making a narrative or signifying architecture. However, as I said before, the formal, programmatic, and performative lessons we learned from this research were able to be transferred to the Mitan project. The narrative research gave it more depth. It is interesting to contrast African art's relation to narrative with the Western canon's move toward abstraction, prompted by its own abstract reading of African art that was itself imbedded with meanings indecipherable to Western culture. So a slave's role has been all too easily erased in the quest for a pure aesthetic.

NR How did your interests in narrative, insertions, and political spatial relationships help formulate your Yale studio on the World Social Forum?

SB While the notion of narrative in architecture has often been framed around the question of "what" architecture communicates, one major interest in the studio was to explore "how" architecture projects. By focusing on mechanisms that are formal, scalar, technological, and so on, the studio focused on architectural questions that were material in nature rather than symbolic or representational. By using the World Social Forum, an organization that denies its "institutionality" and projects itself through its Website yet has an architectural presence, we hoped to create an uncomfortable fit between architecture, institutions, political strategy, and power. In terms of our own practice, especially in working within very specific cultural contexts, we struggle with the relationship of architecture and identity. There is often the pressure for architecture to communicate a clear cultural identity through narrative. We are more interested in the material possibilities and architectural strategies that lead to a clear architectural identity, which is a process that can play itself out uniquely from project to project.

Institution Dissolution

"Architecture is the expression of the very souls of society. Thus great monuments are erected like dikes, opposing the logic and majesty of authority against all disturbing elements. It is in the form of Cathedral or Palace that the church or state speaks to the multitudes and imposes silence upon them."
– Georges Bataille[1]

Architecture and mechanisms of power have long been intertwined and mutually dependent. Political, religious, and commercial institutions have historically invested in building highly orchestrated projections of influence, ideology, and aspiration that bracket and consequently shape much of the public realm. Architecture, in turn, has always relied on the patronage of these institutions, not least their consolidations of capital. Each has supported the advancement of the other, even when the motivations and goals of this partnership have been at odds.

A consequence of the need for governments, churches, corporations, etc., to build architectural monuments that concretize an image of power, solidity, and immortality has been the shaping of places at the architectural and the urban scale. Long before the term *globalization* was coined, the capital that fueled these institutions of power flowed across borders but would then consolidate in certain localities. Georges Bataille's descriptions of palaces and cathedrals and the Modernist skyscraper, office park, and museum were the architectural beneficiaries of these resources. Despite the complexities of financial flows, architecture provided a material presence to "speak to the multitudes," or, as the Bastille posits, a presence that could be targeted by the same horde. Today, the correlation between power and the monumental edifice is not so direct, as ever-more rapid technologies of transaction make the boundaries of institutional entities increasingly difficult to discern. Partnerships between the generators and regulators of capital across borders have blended the interests and often the identities of markets and nation-states. Consequently, architecture's instrumentality as a formal mechanism for projecting institutional power and authority has lost some clarity. Although the recent examples of OMA's CCTV and Coop Himmelblau's ECB are monumental in scale, they are ambiguous in their organizational and formal expression, that is, their representation of an institution of the state, media, or finance.

As institutions of power have become harder to identify, there are fewer Bastilles to storm. Of course, expressions of dissent and resistance sometimes still congregate around buildings. However, architecture has shifted from "target" to "backdrop" as democratic expression becomes increasingly reliant on the media. Furthermore, there is a decreasing relationship between these singular architectural objects and the partnerships that cement monetary, political, and ideological power, as uses often change when the organizations and businesses come and go, such as the Pan Am Building becoming Metropolitan Life. These paradigmatic shifts have required voices of dissent to rethink their tactics and their relationship to institutions and, potentially, architecture.

The World Social Forum (WSF) is a global network of social activists committed to making heard alternative economic, political, social, and environmental viewpoints in its role as a leading organizer of "voices of dissent" to the globe's recent neo-liberal tendencies. It was formed in Brazil in 2001 as "an open meeting place where social movements, networks, NGOs, and other civil society organizations opposed to a world dominated by capital or by any form of imperialism come together to pursue their thinking, to debate ideas democratically, to formulate proposals, share their experiences freely and network for effective action." (www.forumsocialmundial.org). As a response to the World Economic Forum (WEF), its name overtly prioritized human interest over financial interest in guiding global development. In its goals and structure, the WSF has defined itself as a "non-institution," operating as an organizational catalyst rather than as an organization. The WSF is principally a networking mechanism that makes global efforts to counter the WEF's financial capital and cloistered gatherings with human capital and huge, open demonstrations. It does not strive for consensus or specific agendas; the WSF's goal of inclusion is meant to maximize participation.

The headquarters, in São Paulo, Brasil, operates from a 1,000-square-foot office space with fewer then five full-time workers. To have a global presence that belies its minimal human operation, the WSF uses the very same tactics and information technology as the institutions it challenges. Through its Website and networking capabilities, the WSF has a presence in well over a hundred

[1] Georges Bataille, "Architecture," *Oeuvres Completes,* Paris: Gallimard, 1971, p. 171.

countries, with regional offices that operate much like the headquarters. As a coalition of world citizens, the WSF fosters a new form of political space that uses as its model the idea of horizontally structured networks, rather than a hierarchical pyramid. This model reduces points of dispute and facilitates the dynamic of dialogue and collaboration. Thus the virtual community is where the WSF operates, using available and accessible network technologies (the Internet, cell phones, video chat) to construct and maintain a constant, up-to-date dialogue between groups and organizations. The WSF moves out of virtual space to take a visible form a few times a year for the exchange of information in a physical space. The locations for these events change with every meeting, from Mumbai to Porto Allegre, reinforcing the WSF's desire for malleability and immateriality in form. For these moments of solidification, sites are carefully considered because physical presence can produce a singular identity. However, in general, networks are decidedly more important for the WSF than an architectural presence.

While the unwieldy collection of interests and messages generated through these networks is impressive, its effectiveness has been questioned. Can hegemony be countered without a specific agenda or a clear identity? Can productive and comprehensible alternatives be reached in this way? Can the energy of grassroots organizations be consolidated and directed to produce concise and strategic action? Does the nebulous and "non-institutional" presence of the WSF undermine its own effectiveness? While it has taken full advantage of the mechanisms of organization and protest, has the WSF been too quick to dismiss the practicality of a centralized organization that can refine and follow through with counter-initiatives? And, finally, is there a role for architecture in all this? This was the salient and often oxymoronic question put to the studio.

Sunil Bald

BIBLIOGRAPHY

World Social Forum, Website: www.forumsocialmundial .org.br, 2006.

Adorno, Theodor, *The Culture Industry: Selected Essays on Mass Culture,* New York: Routledge, 2001.

Appadurai, Arjun, *Fear of Small Numbers: An Essay on the Geography of Anger,* Durham: Duke University Press, 2006.

Bataille, Georges, "Architecture," *Oeuvres Completes,* Paris: Gallimard, 1971.

Costa, Lucio, *Registro de uma Vivencia,* São Paulo: Empresa des Artes, 1991.

Garcia-Canclini, Nestor, *Hybrid Cultures: Strategies for Entering and Leaving Modernity,* Minneapolis: University of Minnesota Press, 1991.

Hegel, Georg Wilhelm Friedrich, *Aesthetics:* lectures on fine art, volume two, Oxford, Clarendon Press, 1975.

Hollier, Denis, *Against Architecture,* Cambridge: MIT Press, 1988.

Koolhaas, Rem and Mau, Bruce / ed. by Jennifer Sigler, *S, M, L, XL:* Office of Metropolitan Architecture, New York: Monacelli Press, 1998.

Niemeyer, Oscar, "Form and Function in Architecture," *Modulo,* No. 21, 1959.

Sudjic, Deyan, *The Edifice Complex: How the Rich and Powerful Shape The World,* New York : Penguin Press, 2005.

The World Social Forum

After World War II, the United Nations solicited the participation of Modern architects to define a centralized forum for a world political body that could transcend national divisions to work on common global concerns. This studio's mission was to propose a new headquarters for the World Social Forum and its ambitions for affinity over consensus. In doing so, the studio considered the utility and viability of architecture in framing an identity for a body that claims to be "neither a group nor an organization."[2] We are now decades removed from the founding of the UN and the postwar clarity of three worlds with distinct lines drawn between ideologies, governments, and markets. The incongruity of providing an institutional headquarters for this polymorphous network generates a cross-critique of the WSF as well as the relationship of architecture to institutions.

Indeed, when the studio visited the São Paulo office and met with one of the WSF's founders, the premise of the studio was met with an unequivocal "*Não, obrigado!*" ("No, thank you!").

[2] Lucio Costa, quoted in C. R. Dos Santos, *Le Corbusier e o Brasil*, São Paulo: *Projeto*, 1988, p. 178.

COUNTRY, CITY, STREET, SITE

There is no better example of the partnership and patronage of political power and Modern architecture than Brazil. This twenty-five-year trajectory began in 1936 with President Getulio Vargas's commissioning of Lucio Costa to lead a group, including Oscar Niemeyer and Affonso Reidy (with Le Corbusier playing an advisory role), to design the new Ministry of Education in Rio de Janeiro.

Esplanade of the Ministries in Brasília by Richard Niemeyer, 1958.

The Modernist structure projected both monumentality and efficiency, paradigms for the Estado Novo (new state) and the institutionalization of government that marked the country's emergence from colony and oligarchy. In describing the building, Costa emphasized the necessity for institutional architecture to project and formalize an identity and aspiration: "The need to translate in adequate form the idea of prestige and dignity is logically always associated with the public work. This noble intention manifests itself in the monumental proportions of the work and in the simplicity and quality of its finished surfaces."

Avenida Paulista, a five-kilometer road in São Paulo, Brazil.

World Social Forum gatherings and political marches.

and generic structures, toned-down and down-scaled versions of North American models. While there are exceptions such as the Edificio Italia, these buildings sprouted up incessantly in São Paulo, now South America's largest city. São Paulo has always been a commercial city, initially as the center of Brazil's coffee trade and eventually as South America's financial and cultural center. When the national capitol moved to Brasília, Rio de Janeiro became increasingly marginalized as São Paulo exploded in wealth and population.

Unrestricted by a topography like Rio's or a master plan like Brasília's, São Paulo's urban growth sprawled endlessly, with wealthy institutions housed in anonymous glass boxes. Many of the most important companies in South America strove for a presence on Avenida Paulista. An unusually straight avenue in a complex maze of a city, Avenida Paulista runs for almost five kilometers along a high São Paulo ridge. Originally, the avenue was the address of summer mansions of coffee barons who wanted to escape some of the heat and pollution of the downtown only a kilometer below. However, as the city expanded, it became home to bank headquarters and financial institutions, a kind of Brazilian Avenue of the Americas.

The avenue's width and linearity make it a popular setting for both festivals and political marches. It also holds two of São Paulo's best modern buildings: Lina Bo Bardi's Museum of São Paulo and David (not Daniel) Libeskind's Conjunto Nacional. A large empty lot with a dilapidated former mansion on this, South America's richest avenue, provided the ideal site to explore the communicative and formal opportunities of "institutional architecture" for the "non-institutional" WSF.

When the capital was moved from Rio to Brasília a quarter century later, Niemeyer echoed the communicatory and emotive potential of form in the new government buildings: "I am in favor of an almost unlimited plastic freedom… things that are new and beautiful capable of arousing surprise and emotion by their very newness and creativity, designed above all to withdraw the visitor, be it for a few brief instants, from the difficult problems, at times overwhelming, that life poses for all of us."[3]

However, while Brazilian politicians from the municipalities readily engaged so-called strong-form Modernism, private and corporate institutions opted for anonymous

[3] Oscar Niemeyer, "Form and Function in Architecture," *Modulo,* No. 2, 1959, p. 9.

IN SEARCH OF AN ORGANIZATION: WEBSITE

How does one program a "non-institution"? Developing a framework to begin making architecture for an organization that resists it posed a real challenge. We began by looking at the one piece of architecture that projects the WSF body: its Website. As its primary public face, the Website emphasizes the WSF's mission as a site of networking and discourse that denies centralization and the solidification of consensus. And while WSF's primary interface is digital rather than material, the Website is laden with its architectural analogue, which the studio mined to program its architectural analogue.

The students first did tracking analyses, selecting specific concerns of progressive politics following links that began with the Website. This expansion of the portal revealed the organizational dynamics that might begin to influence the structuring of programmatic hierarchies. These tracking analyses were then overlaid with the structure of the site itself. Various taxonomies of concerns, outlined as a handful of "thematic terrains" on the Website, revealed disciplinary categories that could be formalized and networked to each other. Finally, there were program analogues on the Website, that revealed subconscious architectural aspirations about the WSF. "Press Room," "Memorial," and "Library of Alternatives" are links on the site that use architectural metaphors. Mechanisms of information and dissemination began to form a component of the institution that could organize internal terrains while also giving possible public dimensions to the project.

Students were given a document called an "Unbiased Provisional Program," which crossed the Website's tectonic terminology with generic square footages gleaned from a hybridization of multiple institutions, including think tanks, foundations, governmental buildings, etc. The students were then required to both bias and concretize a program by crossing their studies and aspirations with the even and conventional provisional program.

AVENIDA PAULISTA: GLOBAL LOCALITY

The goal of the programming exercise was meant to foreground *bias* over organizational *hierarchy*. The distinction between the two is perhaps subtle, but implicit in bias is a slant that is not necessarily top-down and which often leads to an architectural solution that is bottom-up. Bias also allows the possibility of a simultaneous proposal and critique. In consciously working with bias as an operative conceptual technique, the students could frame their proposals in type, site, institution, or the WSF. Something existing, whether materially or in architectural discourse, was immediately brought into the process.

View of the site from Avenida Paulista, Brazil, in composite panorama, 2006.

Consequently, the first architectural proposal involved working with the site was titled "Of Aggregate Groups and Thematic Terrains." Students were challenged to make an initial formal proposal that might be considered an *inflection* rather than a *construction*. Taking directly from the loose terminology of the WSF, which consciously emphasizes surfaces and connections over boundaries, inflection as a working methodology proposed remaking rather than making, hopefully aligning the WSF's architectural aspirations with its mission as stated on its Website, "Another world is possible."

LEFT Yale students and young Brazilians scaling the concrete dome of Oscar Niemeyer's OCA Folklore Museum in Ibirapuera Park. **RIGHT** View into Estaçao Sé at Praça da Sé subway station, São Paulo, Brazil

RESULTS

In the end, there was great diversity in the students' final architectural proposals and great overlap in their concerns. While categorizing the work is challenging, I have identified the following three strategies of architectural engagement that can be traced to the biases of the students' initial inflection studies:

How is the challenge of a headquarters for the World Social Forum inflected by the multiple urban and public roles of Avenida Paulista? Although São Paulo is notoriously unfriendly to those without cars, it maintains a vibrant street life and is the terrain on which celebrations, demonstrations, and expressions of democracy occur. Four projects defined as *Topological Activism* allowed an activated topology to overtake the project to reformulate the conventional object/landscape binary and, consequently, the conventional binary of public space/institutional space.

How is the generic institutional type, which allows power to be consolidated and operative in secure anonymity, inflected by the organizational aspirations of the WSF? The urban fabric of São Paulo is noticeably lacking in iconic architectural objects. From the midscale corporate towers of Avenida Paulista, where a considerable percentage of the continent's wealth is housed and exchanged, to the proliferating *favelas* that comprise the city's boundaries, these types are generic formally but highly orchestrated organizationally. Three projects use *Stealth Activism* to infiltrate these models and subvert their organizational logic to the advantage of the WSF.

How is the iconic institutional type—which projects an image of power, of monument, which purports to engage the public realm but often operates under Georges Bataille's paradigm—inflected by the non-hierarchal, inclusive rhetoric of the WSF? Brazil has a storied history of concretizing national aspirations through strong formal statements. Three projects, defined here as *Iconic Activism,* use the formal potential of architecture to rethink the notion of an urban iconic object relative to an organization suspicious of power and authority.

MAPPING ANALYSIS

These diagrams mapped where the two opposing organizations, the World Economic
Forum (shown in blue) and the World Social
Forum (red), have held meetings to discuss
the problem of global water scarcity. These
findings were then overlaid on a map locating the areas of the world most affected by
the global shortage. The research revealed
the WEF held larger but fewer meetings in
North America and Europe, areas which are
least affected by the future global shortage.
Conversely, WSF meetings were smaller but
more frequently held in the areas of concern.
The mapping of this single issue reveals an
operational disconnect between the sites of
solution and the sites of problem.

WSF WEB NETWORK

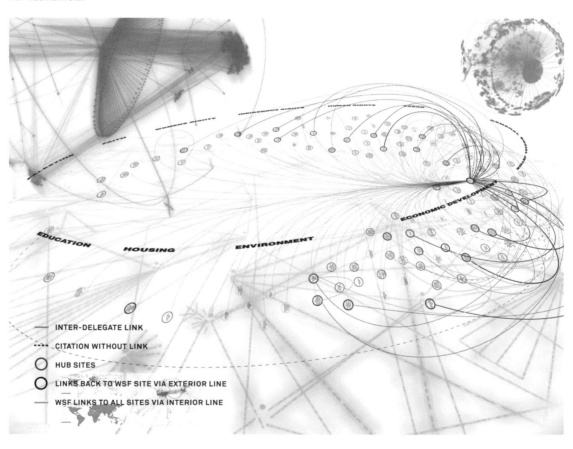

INTER-DELEGATE LINK
CITATION WITHOUT LINK
HUB SITES
LINKS BACK TO WSF SITE VIA EXTERIOR LINE
WSF LINKS TO ALL SITES VIA INTERIOR LINE

The in-bound and outbound links embedded in the WSF Website were graphed
against the group's various areas of activism. The diagram revealed the degree to
which the WSF was overwhelmingly aligned with other groups who held similarly
broad mandates, rather than groups with more specific areas of action. As an
umbrella group, the WSF provides most of its coverage to other "umbrellas."
These general-interest groups form a dense web in which the WSF is a part,
whereas the WSF's hub-and-spoke network with the single-issue activists is
more sparsely populated (George de Brigard and Ross Smith).

MAPPING OF 2005 WORLD ECONOMIC FORUM VERSUS WORLD SOCIAL FORUM RALLIES AND CONFERENCES

WORLD SOCIAL FORUM
(ORGANIZATIONS ADDRESSING
WATER SCARCITY ISSUE)

WORLD ECONOMIC FORUM
(SUEZ: THE WORLD'S LEADING PRIVATE
WATER SERVICES COMPANY)

WATER LEVELS

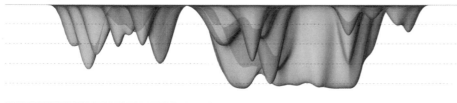

SLIGHT CONCERN

CONCERN

STRESSED

SCARCE

CRISIS

WATER SCARCITY 2025
(POPULATION GROWTH & INFRASTRUCTURE)

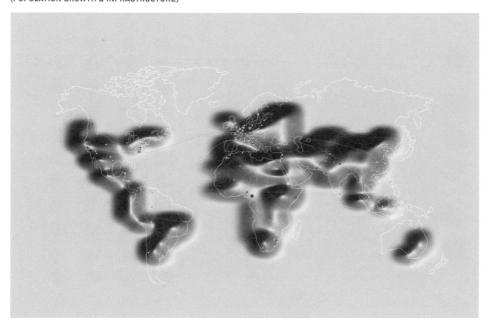

MAPPING OF THEIR RALLIES AND CONFERENCES DURING 2005

JAN – APR   MAY – AUG   SEPT – DEC

Findings were overlaid on a map locating the areas of the world most
affected by the global shortage of water. Research revealed that the
WEF held fewer, larger meetings in North America and Europe, areas
least affected by the future global shortage. Conversely, WSF meetings
were smaller but more frequently held in the areas of concern (Brent
Fleming and Joe Smith).

WSF IN TIME AND SPACE

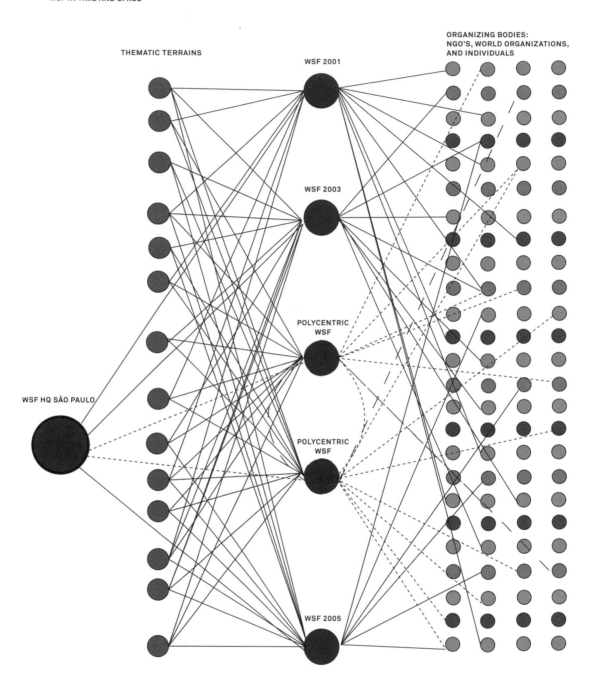

THEMATIC TERRAINS

WSF 2001

ORGANIZING BODIES:
NGO'S, WORLD ORGANIZATIONS,
AND INDIVIDUALS

WSF 2003

POLYCENTRIC
WSF

WSF HQ SÃO PAULO

POLYCENTRIC
WSF

WSF 2005

REVERSING TIME-SPACE RATIO

SPACE

TIME

CURRENT

TIME

SPACE

PROPOSED

Mapping of the WSF terrains and activities (Mayur Mehta).

NATION REPRESENTATION IN THE WSF AND GLOBAL ECONOMY

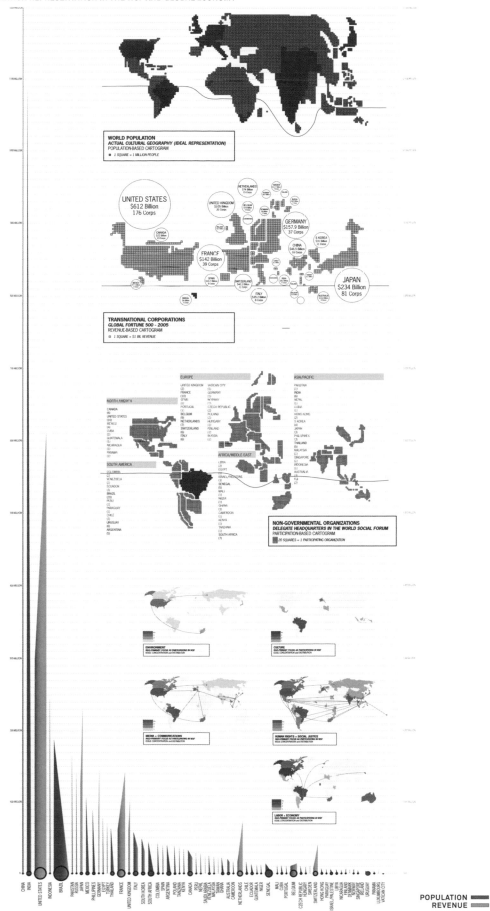

Representational mapping of the WSF delegates by country, population,
and gross national product (Gray Shealy and Heather Kilmer).

1. Stealth Activism

The urban fabric of São Paulo is noticeably lacking in iconic architectural objects. From the midscale corporate towers of Avenida Paulista, where a considerable percentage of the continent's wealth is housed and exchanged, to the proliferating *favelas* that comprise the city's boundaries, these types are generic formally but highly orchestrated organizationally. These three projects infiltrate these models and subvert their organizational logic to the advantage of the WSF.

1.A   Ross Smith

The World Social Forum is an anti-neo-liberal organization which seeks to bring like-minded people together through the organization of social events around the world. Designing a centralized headquarters for this diffused, largely Internet-based organization along São Paulo's most prominent avenue is an exercise in paradox.

Addressing this paradox, Brazil's *favelas* became a precedent for opposing architectural forces in the project. Occupied by Brazil's poor, *favelas* are typical high-rise structures in form but home to a highly organic social condition as they become increasingly occupied by people of little means. In an attempt to capture the organized structural form of the tower but also the chaotic growth of its population, this building project is typical in form but infused with open, unprogrammed public space and landscape. The building thus is appropriate to the mission of the WSF, promoting freewheeling and flexible social organization in its public spaces but also offering an orderly framework in which the events can occur.

1.A.1 Floor plan.

1.A.2 Perspective view of landscaped entry.

1.A.3 Aerial view of site model.

1.A.1

1.A.2

1.A.3

1.A.4 Model of entry plaza.

1.A.5 Programmatic diagram.

1.A.4

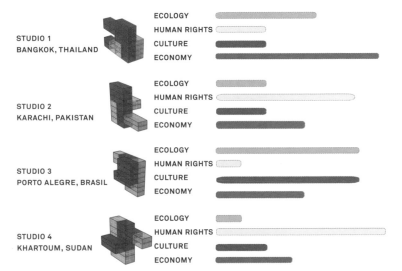

STUDIO 1
BANGKOK, THAILAND

ECOLOGY
HUMAN RIGHTS
CULTURE
ECONOMY

STUDIO 2
KARACHI, PAKISTAN

ECOLOGY
HUMAN RIGHTS
CULTURE
ECONOMY

STUDIO 3
PORTO ALEGRE, BRASIL

ECOLOGY
HUMAN RIGHTS
CULTURE
ECONOMY

STUDIO 4
KHARTOUM, SUDAN

ECOLOGY
HUMAN RIGHTS
CULTURE
ECONOMY

1.A.5

1.A.6 Section through building.

1.A.7 Exterior view of building massing.

1.A.8 Exterior perspective.

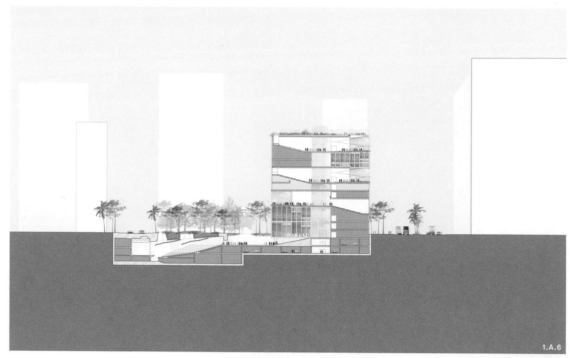

1.A.6

1.A.7

1.A.8

As a completely decentralized organization, the World Social Forum behaves like colonies of like-minded individuals, sharing affinities and networks to create grassroots support for issues surrounding globalization. As such, they represent alternative viewpoints to organizations like the International Monetary Fund, the World Bank, and the G-8. The studio's goal was to design a headquarters for the World Social Forum on Avenida Paulista in São Paulo, home to the largest corporations and banks of Brazil.

The studio posed a central question: how does one center a decentralized organization? This proposal answers that one does not. Though it uses architectural space, the WSF and its affinity organizations seem too ephemeral and temporal to require a headquarters. Rather than provide a center for an organization that wants no identifiable expression or architecture, this proposal seeks to stabilize the program by creating a downtown campus for the Universidade de São Paulo, a social forum that brings these issues for debate to the heart of the financial district of Brazil. In this way, the WSF, its networks, and affinity groups as well as individuals can colonize within a stable environment.

Reef—Individuals using a shared infrastructure
Like a coral reef, the core building provides weather-stabilized vertical topographies that create a variety of spatial experiences and inhabitable spaces. Variation in cross section creates an array of spatial characteristics, from large-scale public performance spaces to small, intimate, or private spaces.

Jellyfish—Individual as collective
Some jellyfish, such as bluebottles, are actually a colony of four different types of organisms that work together to survive and, as for the WSF's cause, express themselves as a single entity. Like a jellyfish, this building consists of four distinct building terrains that can be understood as a single entity: a performance and events center, a media center, a research library, and an interdisciplinary education center. These terrains inhabit different sides of the cross section and overlook each other in longitudinal section. Each individual terrain further breaks down into three distinct zones: individual cells expressed on the façades, glass-louvered enclosed areas at the core for group work, and exterior covered spaces for meetings and activities beyond the scale of the enclosed spaces. Individual primary circulation cores give each terrain autonomy, while secondary circulation provides interconnection between and within terrains.

Leaf Bug—Mimetic among the corporate towers
Surrounded by corporate towers proclaiming singular entities, this building absorbs the built language that surrounds it. Its scale is that of the corporate tower, and the building's expression references existing constructed languages of Avenida Paulista, including massive advertising billboards, communication towers, and bridges among examples of high-rise corporate Modernism.

Dance Steps—Adaptability, movement, and change as constant
Core building programs are arranged when possible as open floor plans, creating large tiers of adaptable space with furniture providing definition to changing programmatic needs. These tiers spill into adjacent covered exteriors. Bridges span from the core space to individual cells, which express the façade and can be expanded into a vertical *favela*.

Transparency—Permeable and sustainable
The building is completely open-air and spatially permeable at grade. Façade screens shade and protect from weather as well as generate electricity. Glass louvers enclose interior spaces but allow for air movement. Sustainability is demonstrated by creating livable environments within climatic extremes and eliminating HVAC systems, except in localized zones requiring air-conditioning (computer labs).

1.B.1 Rendering of building on-site.

1.B.3 Project models.

1.B.4 Elevation showing
programmatic divisions.

1.B.5 Sectional perspective.

1.B.3

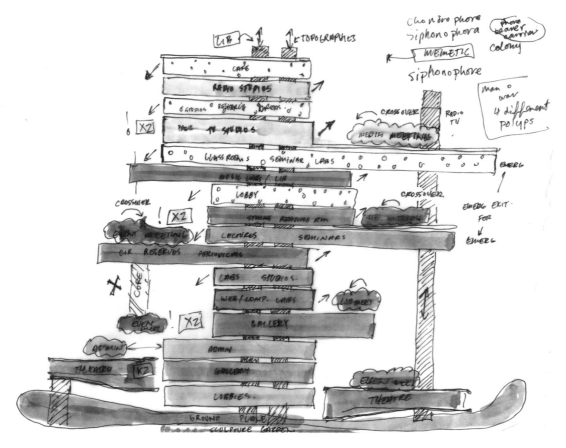

Chondrophore
siphonophora

MIMETIC

siphonophore

phono beaver carrion

colony

man o war
4 different
polyps

1.B.4

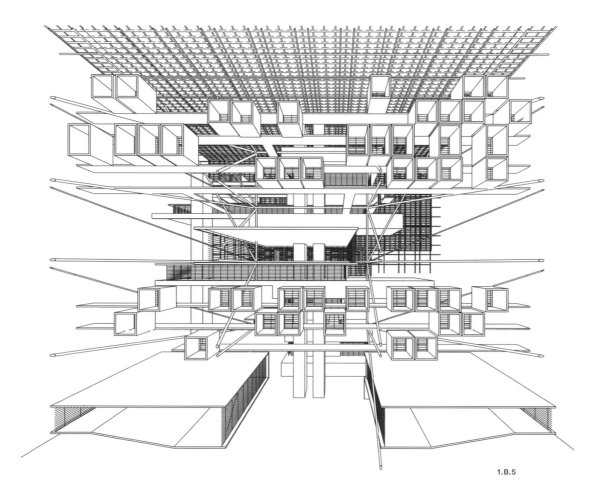

1.B.5

For the World Social Forum, diversity is respected and valued as a strength rather than as a weakness. If another world is possible, "it will be a world in which many worlds fit," said Subcomadante Marcos, leader of the Zapatista resistance. The WSF is completely dependent for its existence upon technology, which recognizes the ever-shifting world, and therefore the WSF treats technology as a mutable infrastructure that can quickly adjust and adapt as needed. In other words, the WSF understands the world as being open and expansive, which is a significant tactical and paradigmatic change that offers an alternative for combating the effects of a neo-liberal capitalist world.

WSF events do have physical spaces of exchange every year in various locations, which change with every meeting, reinforcing the WSF's desire for malleability and immateriality in form. For these moments of solidification, sites are carefully considered, as physical presence can produce a singular identity. Such an identity comes into direct conflict with the multiplicity of WSF's membership. The WSF thinks of itself as the means, not the end. These considerations, for instance, were factored into the WSF's decision to hold its 2003 meeting in an abandoned factory in Mumbai. The selection of a former factory, previously a site of WEF operations, has unmistakable symbolic power and suggests a subversive strategy of infiltration and reprogramming for the critical moments when WSF temporarily assumes physical presence. Given WSF's concerns regarding identity and permanence, designing a "headquarters" for this body is in direct contradiction with its goals and desires. Situating the project on Avenida Paulista, the heart of São Paolo's financial district and the address of a WEF branch, provides an additional layer of complexity.

The design of this project traces the history of public access to the site using the 2003 WSF strategy in Mumbai to reprogram and connect the existing structures through tertiary space. This newly networked place lacks a singular façade but instead re-presents the multiple existing buildings in new, altered states. This transformative process produces a social space that acts as a virtual object in contrast with the other object buildings on Avenida Paulista. This process creates an open and infinitely expandable space that infiltrates and cohabitates with closed corporate space. The first set of diagrams show how the development of transit networks on Avenida Paulista caused shifts in the relationship between public and private spaces. Access to real estate is regulated depending upon the means of movement, whether by foot, car, bus, trolley, subway, or helicopter. This series shows the transformation of the land from open farmland to coffee-baron mansions to corporate headquarters. The site contains a fragment from each of these eras: an abandoned early-twentieth-century mansion at the front of the lot, a new tower clad in blue glass behind the mansion, and closed park surrounded by a wall. A newsstand sits on the corner of the lot next to a bus stop, thirty feet above the subway beneath the avenue.

The second set of diagrams implement the infiltration and re-appropriation strategy of Mumbai; deprogramming and reprogramming begins along the periphery of the tower and continues around to the mansion and on to the newsstand. New program becomes inserted below grade to connect these object buildings. Classrooms, offices, a gallery, a library, a new subway stop, an auditorium, a production studio, a media center, a café, a kitchen, showers, and changing rooms encircle and support a central event space. This space is open twenty-four hours a day for performances and rallies and sets aside areas for a garden, *fiera*, and campground. The "building" exists on the periphery, without a central structure above or below ground, thus inverting the dominant object-in-field organization typically found on Avenida Paulista. By reversing the field/object, historical accessibility is also reversed: private becomes public. The project for the World Social Forum Headquarters uses this interstitial programming to support a virtual-object space that is flexible and responsive to the needs of the perimeter.

1.C.1   Plans, existing, roof plan, and first sub floor .

1.C.2   Existing condition, proposed intervention with central event space.

1.C.3   Below-grade connections of existing structures.

1.C.4   Section through subway, library, and administration offices.

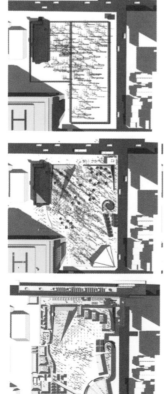

1.C.1

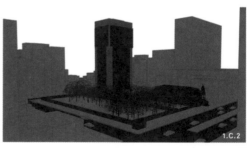
1.C.2

1.C.3

1.C.4

1.C.5 World Social Forum event in progress.

1.C.6 Section through subway station, library, and news-stand entry.

1.C.5

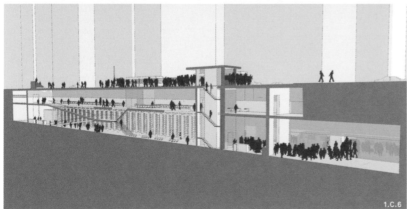

1.C.6

1.C.7 Diagram of the development of transit networks on Avenida Paulista, which caused shifts in the relationship between the public and private spaces.

1.C.8 Diagram implements the infiltration and re-appropriation strategy of Mumbai; deprogramming and reprogramming begins along the periphery in the tower and continues around to the mansion and on to the newsstand, forming the central event space.

1.C.9 By reversing the field/object, historical accessibility is also reversed: private becomes public. The project for the World Social Forum Headquarters uses this interstitial programming to support a virtual-object space that is flexible and responsive to the needs of the perimeter.

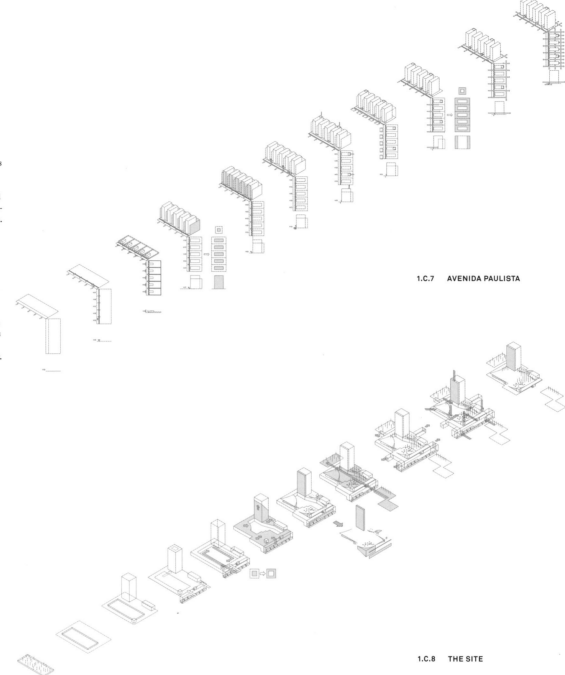

1.C.7   AVENIDA PAULISTA

1.C.8   THE SITE

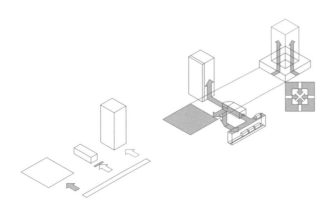

1.C.9   THE SOLUTION

Topological Activism

Although São Paulo is notoriously unfriendly to those without cars, it maintains a vibrant street life and is the terrain on which celebrations, demonstrations, and expressions of democracy occur. These three projects allow an activated topology to overtake the project to re-formulate the conventional object/landscape binary and consequently the conventional binary of public space/institutional space.

David Nam 2.A

The design for the World Social Forum Headquarters addressed two primary concerns: architecture and its capacity to represent a social institution, and how architectural program might be judged by performance effectiveness.

Through research on the architecture and performance of think tanks, a correlation was discovered between the organizational models of networked organizations such as the WSF and the operational effectiveness of multidisciplinary institutions such as RAND. The spatial organization of RAND's first headquarters, in Santa Monica, California, was designed to promote increased collaboration among its many departments; the selection of a lattice-like plan was based on calculations for maximizing chance encounters and interactions among the researchers of differing disciplines.

Conceiving of the WSF as a think tank made sense. It would operate as a permanent meeting spot and workplace for developing the ideas initiated at the annual WSF events. As a think tank, the activities of the WSF encompassed research, public events, culture, education, press, and youth programs. An analysis of the minimum area per person was performed on each of the components of the program, establishing a scenario for occupancy density. These densities were distributed to promote overlaps and juxtapositions, engendering activities that would continually reference each other, thereby promoting increased dialogue among the users and an active occupation of the building.

2.A.1 Sectional perspective.

2.A.2 East-west section.

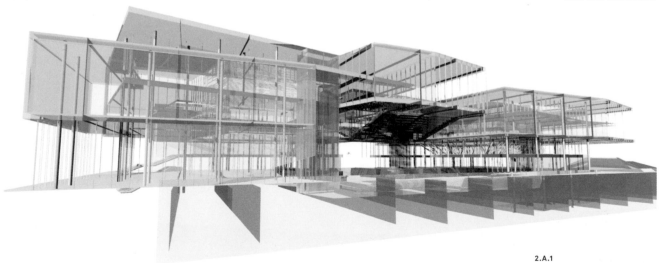

2.A.1

2.A.2

2.A.3 Preliminary surface studies.

2.A.4 Rendering showing site and context.

2.A.5 Final model.

CENTRALIZED

DECENTRALIZED

DISTRUBUTED NETWORK

2.A.6

DISTRIBUTED NETWORK DIFFERENTIATED AS AGGREGATES

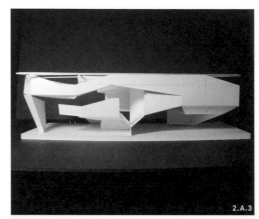

2.A.3

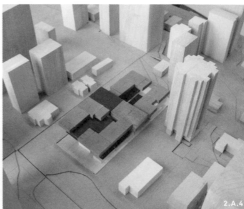

2.A.4

2.A.5

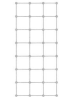 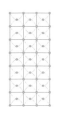 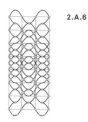 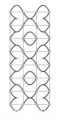

2.A.6

2.A.6 Organizational model diagrams from Paul Baran, RAND Corporation, 1964.

2.A.7 Programmatic distribution of activity mixing swarm theory with activation.

2.A.8 Programmatic layering and massing.

UNDIFFERENTIATED DISTRIBUTED NETWORK

NEW FORMATIONS WITHIN DISTRIBUTED NETWORK

AGGREGATIONS WITHIN DISTRIBUTED NETWORK

AGGREGATIONS ENABLING NEW FORMATIONS WITHIN DISTRIBUTED NETWORK

GROUND LEVEL   LEVEL 1   LEVEL 2   LEVEL 3   LEVEL 4

  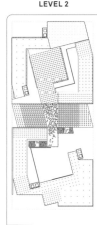  

2.A.7

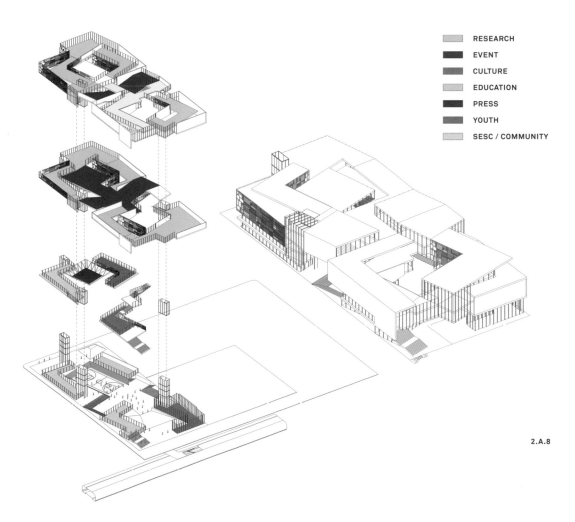

RESEARCH
EVENT
CULTURE
EDUCATION
PRESS
YOUTH
SESC / COMMUNITY

2.A.8

Tourism has been the World Social Forum's primary tool to annually bring together people at polycentric venues to sponsor dialogue, protests, and legal action. The identity of the WSF is solidified in the manner in which it disseminates information on a global scale. Essentially, the WSF has created its own brand of so-called issue-based tourism, which gathers people around a political or socioeconomic agenda. In this project, free assembly has resolved itself into a transient hotel, a temporal gathering area that allows social interaction in a twenty-four-hour urban zone. As a historically political space in chaotic countries, the hotel becomes a tool for political action.

The hotel occupies the site as a multistoried, horizontal, democratic, and accessible landscape, acknowledging the anti-corporate, "anti-Avenida Paulista" agenda of the WSF. Central to the concept is the hybridization of the hotel room and the temporal World's Fair-like fairground, in which pavilions are used as tools for the dissemination of information. After considering the topography of the site, it was decided the project should include an existing grove of trees as a significant feature. Thus, the building weaves around the trees, acknowledging them as an important ecology.

The objective of the hotel is to use its common spaces as a social condenser: rooms are centered around social clusters distributed throughout the hotel, which fosters discussion as part of this twenty-four-hour space. The thematic terrains below are layered topographic levels that function somewhat like a traditional conference area: events based around central WSF issues are hosted on various internal and external levels throughout the year. Delegate NGOs are allotted gallery, office, and meeting space, as well as the use of indoor and outdoor forums to spread information, foster ideas, and organize protests. The second level hosts Tent City: participants construct temporary pavilions using the architecture as a framework in the creation of a fairground. The hotel rooms above nod to this temporal landscape, as they are conceptualized as temporary structures realized in rigid fabric over the permanent skeleton. In this way, the hotel room itself becomes a space for habitation, exhibition, and discussion—a political engine that gets to the core of the WSF mission of gathering people to foster ideas.

2.B.1 View of project from Avenida Santos during forum.

2.B.2 Photograph of sectional model showing section cut from Avenida Santos.

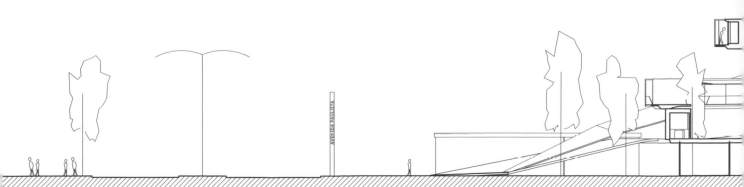

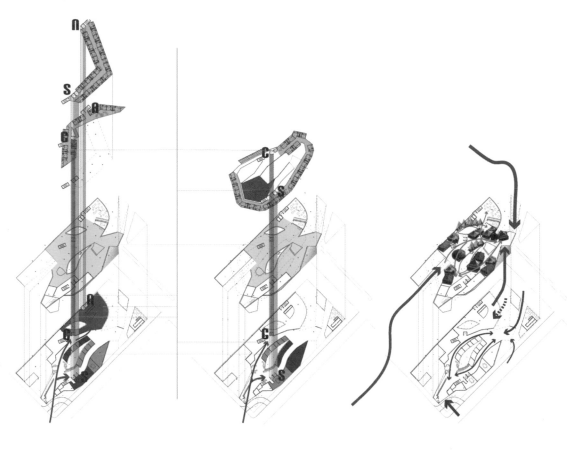

2.A.3 Programmatic diagram showing multivenue capacity of the project.

2.A.4 Comparison of inhabitation diagrams of resorts, hotels, and markets juxtaposed on topographic limitations of the site. This analysis was used to generate form and programmatic placement in the project.

2.A.5 Sectional drawing showing major axis from Avenida Paulista to Avenida Santos.

TERRAIN A

HUMAN RIGHTS NGOS
ENVIRONMENT DELEGATES
WSF POLYCENTRIC EVENT
BRAZILIAN LANDLESS PEOPLES
POST CONFLICT DIALOGS

TERRAIN B

CULTURAL REPRESENTATIVES (SE ASIA NGO)
MEDIA / COMMUNICATIONS DELEGATES
WSF POLYCENTRIC EVENT
LABOR / ECONOMIC DELEGATES
AMERICAN ENVIRONMENT SUMMIT

COLONIZED TERRAIN / FLOWS

2.B.3

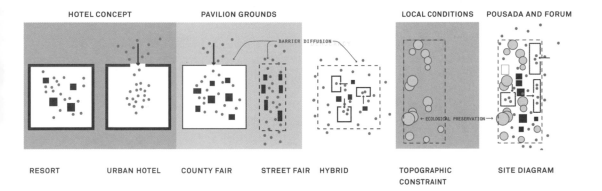

HOTEL CONCEPT

PAVILION GROUNDS

LOCAL CONDITIONS   POUSADA AND FORUM

BARRIER DIFFUSION

← ECOLOGICAL PRESERVATION →

RESORT   URBAN HOTEL   COUNTY FAIR   STREET FAIR   HYBRID   TOPOGRAPHIC   SITE DIAGRAM
                                                                             CONSTRAINT

2.B.4

2.B.5

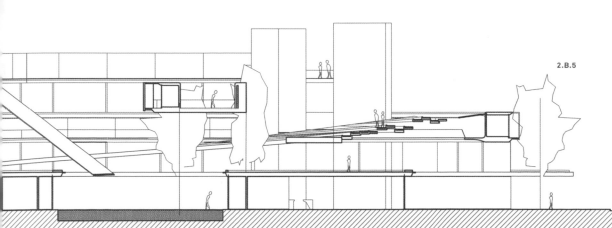

Avenida Paulista, the future site of the World Social Forum Headquarters, is at the heart of São Paulo and South America's business and commercial district. This contentious site is dominated by South America's largest private corporations, the missions of which are antithetical to the WSF's. These institutions are housed in skyscrapers (restricted from the general public) and compete to erect ever-taller buildings. Rather than "fitting in" with its corporate high-rise neighbors, the WSF Headquarters in this proposal is explored as being itself an overt protest of the dominant architectural form and accessibility found along Avenida Paulista, explicitly proclaiming itself as idiosyncratic or "other."

Public Landscape
São Paulo's subtropical climate allows opportunities for architectural reinvention. The mild climate has an exterior thermal comfort zone approximately seventy-five percent

of the year. Intense sun during the high summer months is the major source of thermal discomfort. With adequate shade and ventilation, the facility for the WSF can comfortably be an extension of the public landscape. Rather than closing off the building to the public, a topological surface weaves throughout the building; it never closes or is off-limits to the public. As the surface undulates, it creates enclosures to house programs that need acoustic clarity or functional privacy. Space within the building is often hybrid space and cannot be classified as "interior" or "exterior," which encourages new types of inhabitation, exploration, occupation, and playfulness within the architecture. This casual and relaxed atmosphere precludes the architectural conventions along Avenida Paulista, and its mutability is characteristic of the WSF. In that spirit, the building's design makes use of horizontality and unrestrictedness, rather than verticality and exclusivity.

2.C.1 World Social Forum as urban public space.

2.C.2 Aerial view of World Social Forum Headquarters.

2.C.3 Massing study model.

2.C.4 Massing study model.

2.C.1

2.C.2

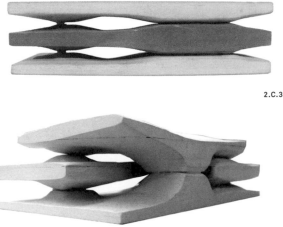

2.C.3

2.C.4

PROGRAMMATIC DISTRIBUTION

ACCESS
    PUBLIC SURFACE
    SEMI PUBLIC SPACES
    PRIVATE SPACES

2.C.5 Diagram of programmatic distribution and levels of building access.

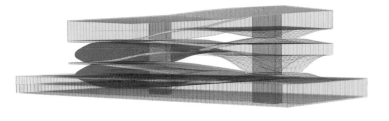

WORLD SOCIAL FORUM
    PUBLIC SURFACE THROUGHOUT BUILDING
    PUBLIC DEMONSTRATION AREA
    SEMI PUBLIC EVENT, FACULTY SUPPORT SPACES
    PRIVATE OFFICES AND MEETING AREAS

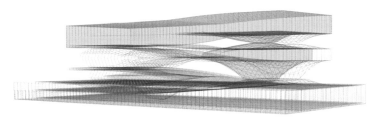

FLUID IDEOLOGICAL TERRAINS
    OFFICE SPACE
    RESEARCH
    MEETING AND CONFERENCE ROOMS

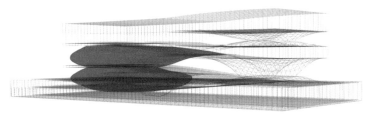

EVENT SPACES
    AUDITORIUM
    DEMONSTRATION OR PUBLIC GATHERING SPACE

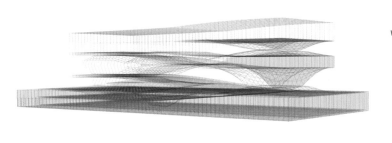

WSF ADMINISTRATIVE SPACES
    WELCOME CENTER
    INFORMATION OFFICE
    ADMINISTRATIVE OFFICES
    CONFERENCE ROOMS
    SUPPORT SPACES

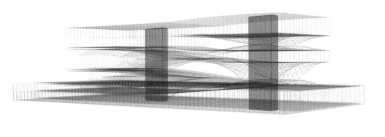

CIRCULATION CORES
    ELEVATORS
    EGRESS STAIRS
    PUBLIC AND PRIVATE FACILITIES

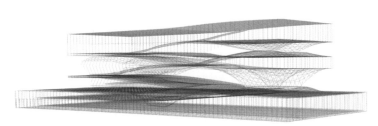

PUBLIC TOPOLOGICAL SURFACE
    CIRCULATION RAMP
    ROOF GARDENS
    PUBLIC PARKS

2.C.5

2.C.6 Circulation diagram.

2.C.7 Structural diagram.

2.C.8 Building section.

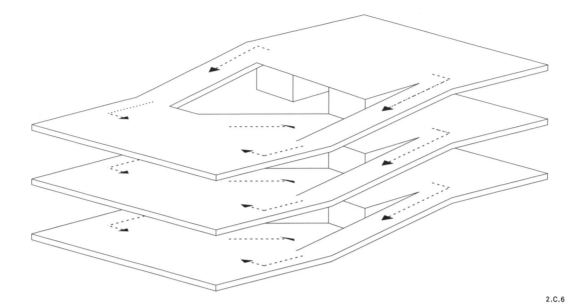

2.C.6

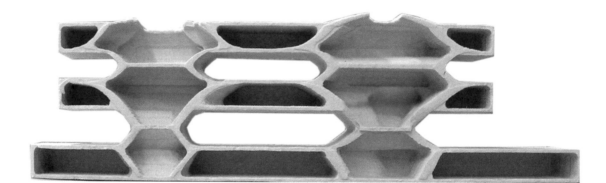

2.C.7

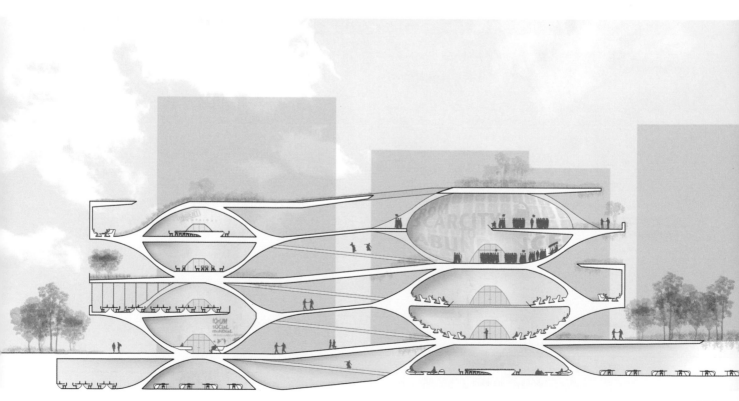

2.C.8

The WSF studio project is a response to two key issues: the problems faced by attendees of the WSF due to the overwhelming scale of its annual events, and the limiting nature of a physical building for the organization's needs in general.

Conceived as a permanent protest stage, this project reverses the time-space relationship of the existing format of the WSF event, allowing for a continuous dialogue against neo-liberalism, a key concern of the WSF committee. This inversion of the time-space category is achieved by dedicating a series of permanent spaces that would be used simultaneously across the world for this event, eliminating a temporal format of one place at one time. Unlike the current framework of the WSF event, which takes place over a period of a few days every year in a conference-like setting at one specific place, this project proposes a São Paulo FORUM as a model for centers spread across urban regions of the world, extending the polycentric effort of the 2006 WSF event into a permanent vision.

Responding to the committee's aversion to institutionalizing the organization through a typical building that serves as a standardized and stagnant headquarters, the project reevaluates the controlling and dissecting nature of buildings. Lifted above the ground plane, the FORUM building allows for people to cross the adjacent streets while simultaneously allowing for multiple stages for public protest within and below the structure. Located on São Paulo's most important business avenue and packed with financial institutions and corporate headquarters, the building forms the perfect stage for demonstrations and rallies against capitalist ventures and architecturally confronts them in its physical and altered presence.

Evaluating the overwhelming scale of the main event brought to light some key logistical concerns—such as disorientation due to the physical expanse of the event and cordoning off large areas in the city—and an overwhelming influence of specific thematic terrains through each event. By inverting the time-space equation, the new FORUM allows for topics or incidents of immediate relevance to be discussed at their time of occurrence. Instead of a large-scale event in a short span of time, it will be a small event not limited by time and emphasizing spontaneity. By dedicating a part of the city for this continuous event, organized protests can be held in an easily maneuverable space at the heart of the city.

The building comprises five components: the research zone, the youth hostel, the media zone, and the administrative area, which are all stitched together by the meeting/protest areas spread across the building. Adjacencies across programmatic components are based on easy access between specific functions. A protest ramp forms the building's front façade, channeling protesters along Avenida Paulista into the building plot. Theatrical in its endeavor, the ramp travels up along the periphery of the plot boundary and gives a clear view of protests and demonstrations, which have direct access to the building from every bounding street, culminating in an architecturally framed stage at the upper level facing the main avenue. The transparent nature of the FORUM building enables it to become an appropriate city stage for protests and rallies supporting the agendas of the World Social Forum. A second protest stage is located at the lower-level amphitheater for gatherings at a much larger scale. Formed by a series of terraces and a main platform below, the amphitheater acts literally and metaphorically as a collector of protestors. In combination with the open space at the ground level, the amphitheater doubles as a public city space during periods of non-demonstration.

A key driver for the project was to decentralize the event to allow for the free exchange of ideas across different parts of the world. The World Wide Web will play a significant role in making the FORUM a successful channel for the flow and exchange of ideas among WSF centers, thus emphasizing a decentralized, perpetually active organization. Teleconferencing and projection cameras, spread across the public space of the FORUM building to simulcast events occurring in other WSF centers, result in a truly continuous field of information.

While the nature of protest has historically been to disrupt daily life, the FORUM is a platform to discuss and demonstrate in order to be heard and seen without causing dysfunction in the city. The current format of the WSF events enables dialogue; however, there have been few solutions to the matters being discussed. The temporal character of the event could be one reason for the lack of any resolution to the issues under investigation. The new FORUM will allow for such matters to be discussed at length, creating the possibility of finding solutions or courses of action.

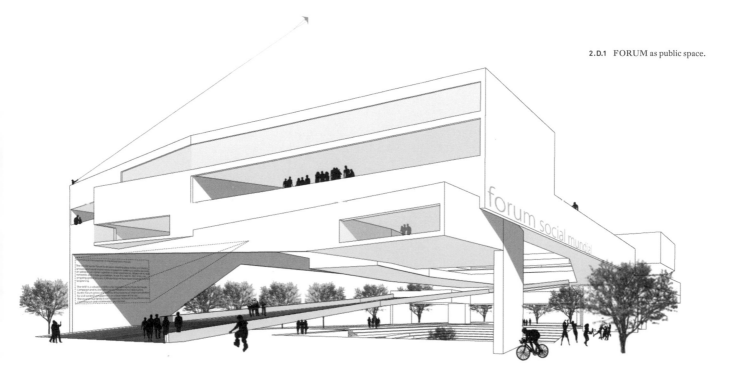

2.D.1 FORUM as public space.

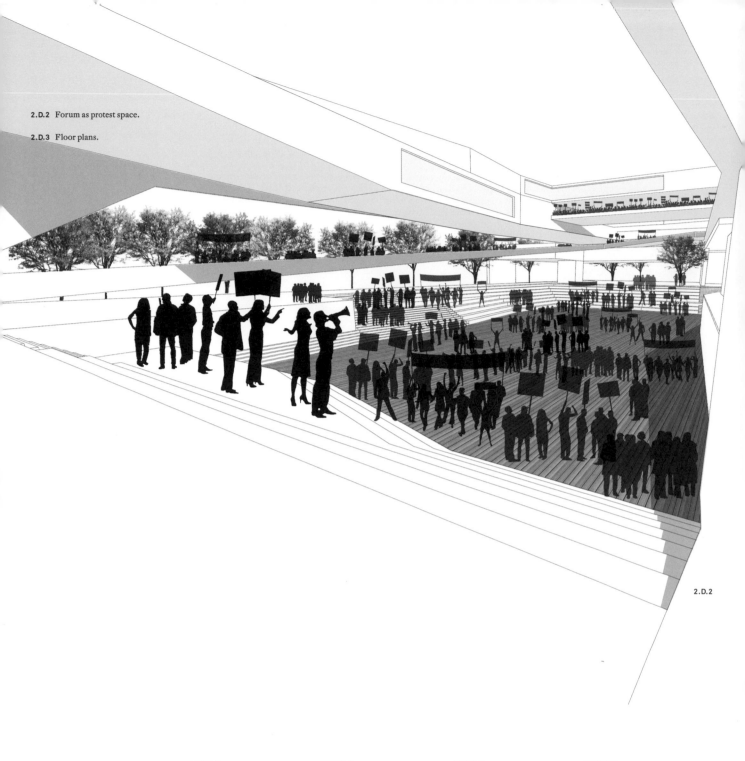

2.D.2 Forum as protest space.

2.D.3 Floor plans.

2.D.2

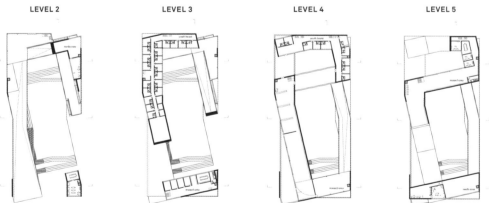

LEVEL 2   LEVEL 3   LEVEL 4   LEVEL 5

2.D.3

2.D.4 Programmatic adjacencies and area distribution.

2.D.5 Appropriating the built form.

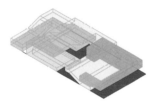

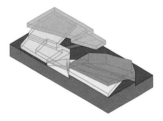

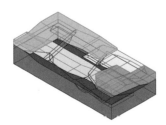

2.D.4

2.D.5

3. Iconic Activism

Modernist architecture has long played a role in concretizing Brazil's national aspirations through strong formal statements. The next three projects use the formal potential of architecture to think about the notion of an iconic urban object relative to an organization suspicious of power and authority.

3.A   Frank Melendez

3.A.1 Sectional study model.

3.A.2 Exterior view of World Social Forum Headquarters.

Through an analysis of the World Social Forum's philosophy, this project attempts to generate an architectural condition that responds to the local and global conditions of the organization. The proposed building is split into two types of space: embedded and fluid. The embedded spaces respond to the local conditions of the project's site, São Paulo's Avenida Paulista, the cultural identity of Brazil and a site of traditional building materials and techniques. The fluid spaces respond to the global WSF organization, the digital space that it occupies, and its extensive network of individuals and groups.

Conceptually, the embedded spaces consist of three faceted "rocks" that have been dropped into a high-viscosity liquid, a fluid space. The rocks are assigned programmatic functions such as enclosed theaters for music and dance, seminar rooms, and event rooms, while the fluid spaces contain Web-access areas, large, open gathering spaces, and art galleries. By reassigning and shifting programmatic hierarchies, new programs and spaces emerge, such as digital media rooms, Internet stations, a book library, art studios, and performance areas. The resulting architecture is composed of a series of solids and voids that overlap and braid to form a homogeneous space. Only traces of the embedded and fluid spaces remain, while the interstitial space becomes the new rhizomatic structure, building typology, and form.

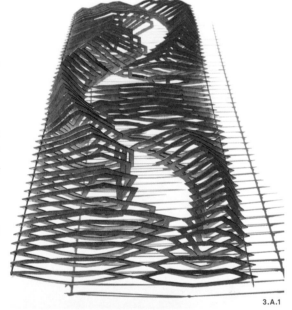

3.A.1

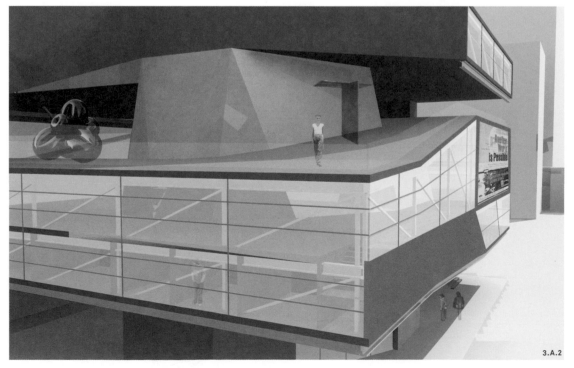

3.A.2

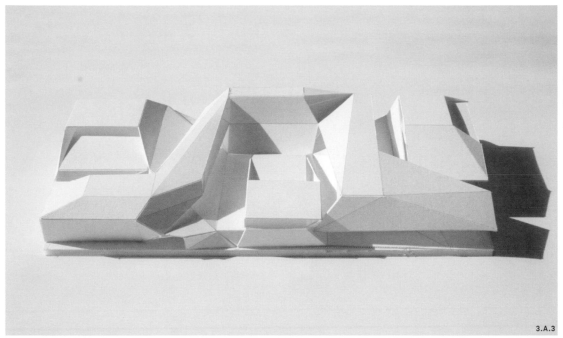

3.A.3 Volume studies.

3.A.4 Massing-model renderings.

3.A.5 Building plans and sections.

3.A.3

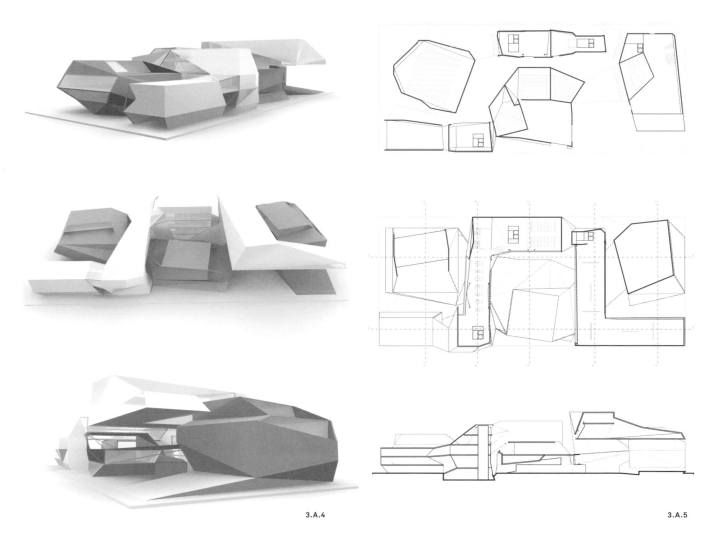

3.A.4

3.A.5

3.A.6 Study models and programmatic distribution.

PROGRAM DISTRIBUTION:
EMBEDDED SPACES

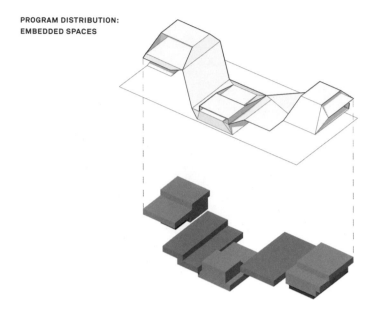

PROGRAM DISTRIBUTION:
FLUID SPACES

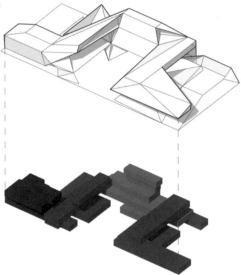

TOTAL PROGRAM
DISTRIBUTION

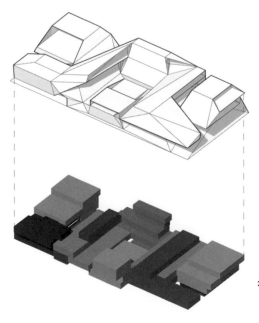

3.A.6

The World Social Forum is an organization that attempts to galvanize worldwide attention and support for progressive ideas and institutions across the globe. It is an Internet-based, anti-hierarchical body that, with a full-time staff of only three people, manages to sponsor the assembly of hundreds of thousands of people each year. Based in São Paulo, FORUMs have been held in Porto Alegre, Brazil, Caracas, Venezuela, Bamako, Mali, and Mumbai, India.

Through analytic exercises and research in the early stages of the studio, I became interested in issues of projection and what its implications were for the WSF. Beyond its technical meaning with regard to architecture, the term has connotations in performance, broadcasting, and statistics, among other topics, which is evocative when grappling with the problem of the WSF. Finally, the asymmetric relationship between source and receiver provided an apt metaphor for the WSF and its activities.

The ability of the WSF staff to do so much with so little called into question the utility and function of a headquarters. At the same time, the massive scale of the FORUM events themselves threatened to overwhelm the site on Avenida Paulista, at the heart of São Paolo's banking and corporate culture. Projection, as a means of enlarging, reducing, focusing, communicating, and even surveying, provided both a means to approach the project intellectually and a formal system by which to organize architectural conclusions.

From the exterior, the design is a crisp, opaque block raised off the group to create a shaded plaza beneath the entire headquarters. Incisions running up the façade make the faceted areas of the glass curtain wall recessed. The interaction between activity in the building's interior and activity on the city streets outside occurs at the resulting oblique angles.

Similarly glazed and opaque surfaces line the atria that penetrate the solid block, allowing views across the building, between different program areas and between people gathering on the plaza and those inside the headquarters. These voids are used to divide programmatic areas within the building without creating disruptive or inflexible lines of demarcation. Programs can grow and recede around the atria voids, while the open ends and transparent atria allow for collaboration and interaction. The size of the atria and the spaces between them are scaled across the site to filter and organize activities within the building by their degree of intimacy. In section, floor plates that bend seamlessly into connecting ramps reinforce the openness and flexibility of the headquarter's interior by combining with the voids of the atria to produce an open-celled network of spaces.

This project's goal was to take a handful of material and organizational conventions from the São Paolo context—e.g., the imposing concrete of the corporate towers and mall-like ground floors of many buildings that Paulistas use to avoid the intense sun—and apply a formal system to create a headquarters responsive to the flexible nature of the WSF. This approach should be seen as a rejection of any attempt to produce a physical manifestation of the WSF ideology, an exercise that would necessarily involve codifying the group's mission in a way that is antithetical to its goals. Using projection both as an organizational approach and a formal technique opened up an opportunity to use a small vocabulary of design processes in the creation of a building whose inhabitants' activities will provide substantial richness to the form. Rather than creating a building-as-critique, the building returns the critical mandate to the WSF while remaining an active and intriguing construction.

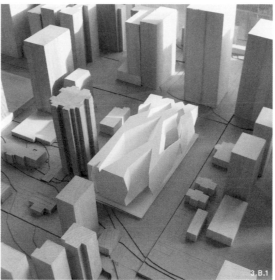

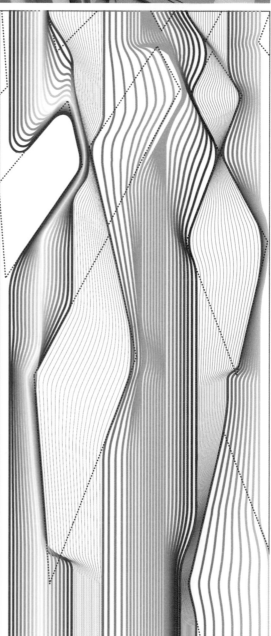

3.B.1 Aerial photograph of model.

3.B.2 Analysis of striated and fluid programs.

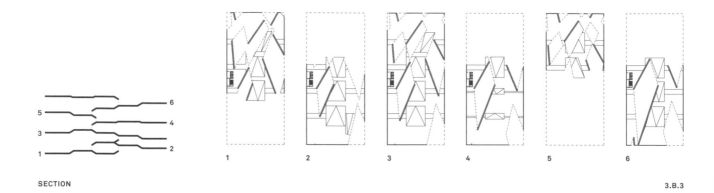

SECTION

1 2 3 4 5 6

3.B.3

3.B.4

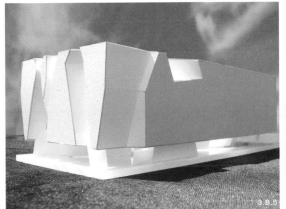

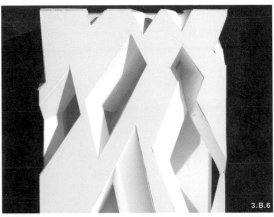

3.B.5

3.B.6

3.B.7

3.B.3 Program activities are arranged in the building by using the atria and sectional changes as a filter to capture and suspend various activities. Occupants, meanwhile, can circulate freely among program elements.

3.B.4 View of the plaza that extends under the entire building. The intense sunlight of this latitude creates alternating pools of light and shadow while allowing visual connections between the public and inner spaces of the building.

3.B.5 Model photograph. The WSF Headquarters presents itself as both a regular form and an irregularly composed façade.

3.B.6 Model photograph in site from the southeast. Unlike the concrete towers surrounding the site, the WSF Headquarters is set back from Avenida Paulista.

3.B.7 Interior rendering. View across one of the atria. The irregular geometry of each atrium provides unexpected sight lines within the building and in the plaza. Connections can be made between activities of any of these participants; the sense of institutional openness is highlighted in the process.

While a Website of the World Social Forum provides it with a consistent virtual presence, the organization's physical presence remains fluid: each year, a forum event composed of thousands of people from around the world descends on a city, such as Bombay or Davos. This project's urban strategy is to create an architectural object that provides an institutional identity for the WSF Headquarters while also expressing the irony of its location and the need for any kind of permanence. Programmatically, the project uses the fluid nature of the organization as a way to reconsider institutional space, in which program is typically compartmentalized. Instead of overlaying program onto the site, program is invented through the interaction of landscape and a fluid spine that runs the length of the site. The fluid spine serves as a programmatic armature that breaks the institutional framework by short-circuiting the larger zones.

3.C.1 Programmatic organization and circulation. Streams of program flow through the site, intersecting and interacting while defining fields that can accommodate open programs, such as galleries and event spaces. The streams are manipulated to accomodate a density of program of different types along with circulation. The convergence of streams creates a density in the center of the site, while the periphery remains porous.

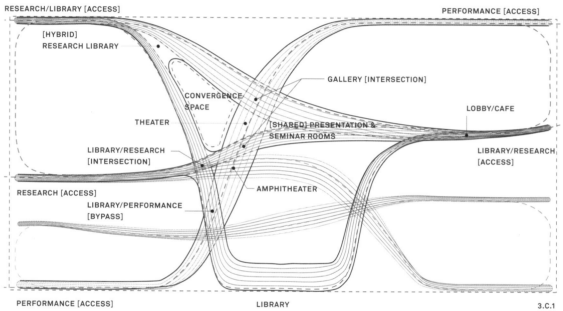

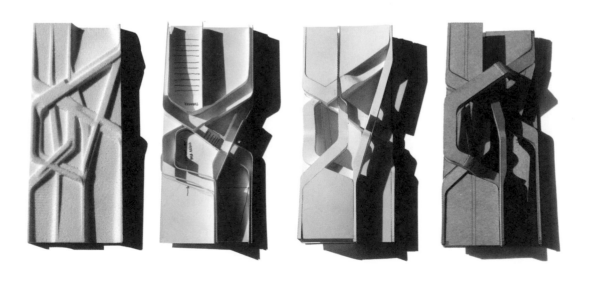

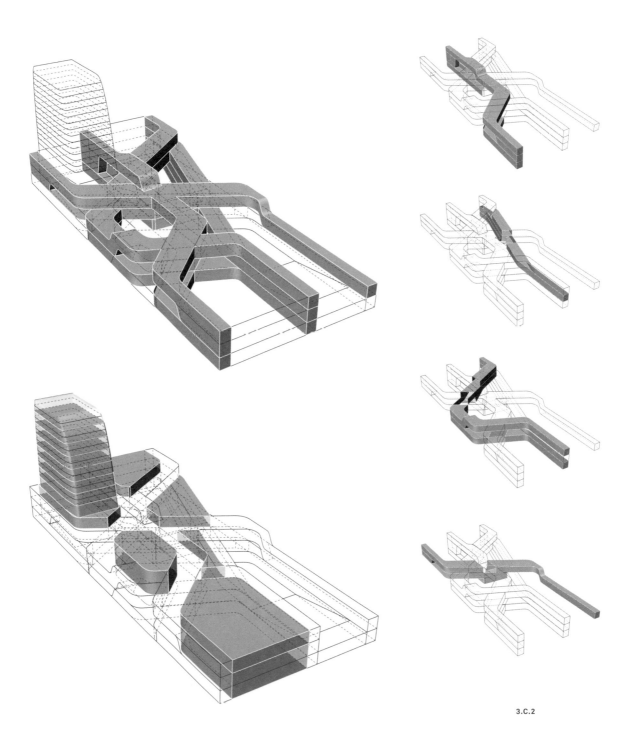

3.C.2

3.C.3 Site and floor plans.

3.C.4 Interior perspectives.

3.C.5 Exterior perspectives.

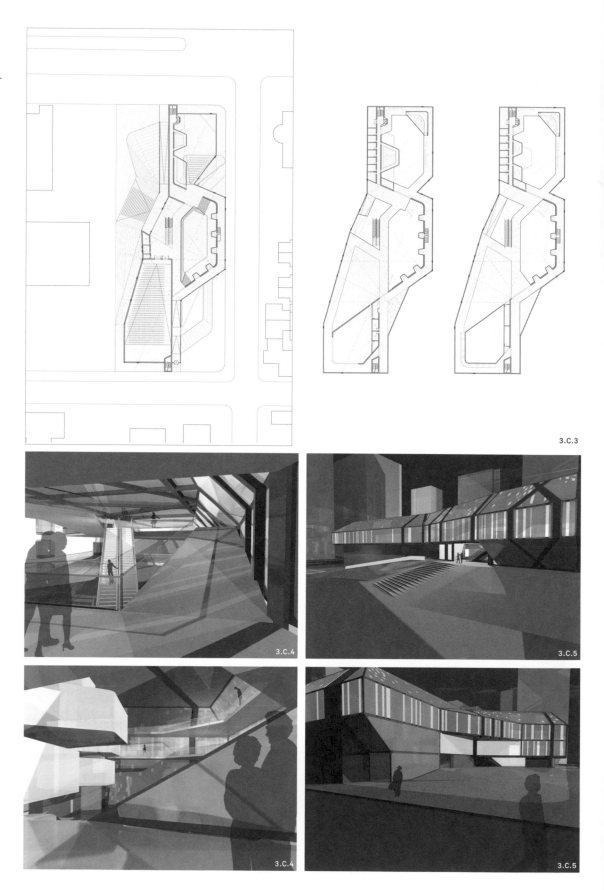

3.C.3

3.C.4

3.C.5

3.C.4

3.C.5

3.C.6

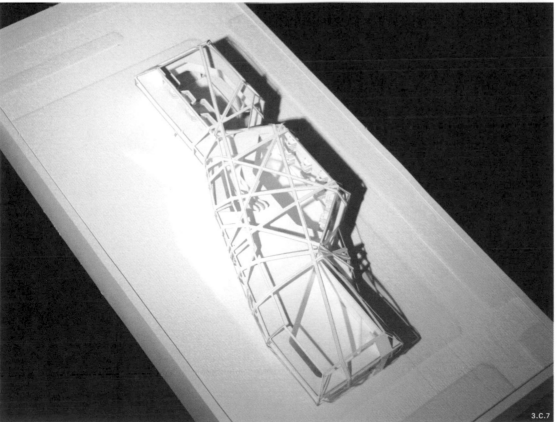

3.C.7

Marc Tsurumaki

AMPHIBIOUS TACTICS

AN INTERVIEW WITH Marc Tsurumaki

NINA RAPPAPORT I am interested in how your New York architecture practice, Lewis.Tsurumaki.Lewis, transitions from critical theoretical projects
to built work. For instance, I see one aspect of your work as tweaking
the norm and making people stop to think about the world they inhabit.
How do you reinterpret that kind of criticality in a functional building?

MARC TSURUMAKI That is a question that we are conscious of because we
principally had been doing speculative projects that were textually and
graphically or drawing-based. In that context we had a lot of time to think
and theorize, which is incredibly useful at one stage. Fortunately we
became busy with real projects and shifted into a period of heavier production, without as much time to be self-conscious. But we hope the transition
isn't that radical because, even in the theoretical work, we were interested
in examining real-world conditions—as you say, tweaking and distorting
or recombining normative conditions to produce unprecedented speculative ones. As we have moved more into commissioned and built projects,
it is sometimes a challenge to maintain the same degree of speculation or
invention because of the inevitable pressures of time, budget, and program.
On the other hand, our methodological approach, whether in the context
of self-generated or commissioned work, is really one of a creative engagement within limits and the way these very limits can become the catalyst
for design invention. In the earlier, speculative work, this had a lot to do
with investigations into the economical, logistical, social, technological,
and political conditions—which are inevitably embodied in the conventions
of architecture—and how these tend to generate a set of provisional typological operations. In the built work, this method often results in a tactical
focus on a limited number of parameters, which we see as potentially
productive, asking ourselves, "What are the most relevant constraints?"
By its very nature the architectural project is constrained by a whole
network of external forces. What we attempt to do is maneuver opportunistically within those constraints rather than oppose those forces.

NR How does this negotiating transpire in the design and construction
of small restaurants around New York City, where you have had to deal
with the constraints of time, program, and space as well as cost? If your
early speculative work looked at conventions of program and spatial
typology, how do you transfer that to the physicality of materials to
exploit them in new ways?

PREVIOUS PAGE Lewis.Tsurumaki.Lewis,
Memorial Sloan-Kettering, art installation,
New York, 2009.

LEFT Lewis.Tsurumaki.Lewis, Arthouse at
the Jones Center, Contemporary Art Museum,
Austin, Texas, rendering, 2009.

MT We realized quickly that the opportunities in the restaurants tended not to be in the plan or overall spatial configurations, which were in large part dictated by considerations of efficiency. In all those projects we were dealing with relatively confined spaces within pre-existing buildings, as well as the limits of the envelope we were given. This situation meant the primary site for operation shifted to the surfaces of the space–the thin zone six inches from the wall, the ceiling, or the floor. This constraint produced an opportunity, namely, to engage and invent surfaces through the aggregation of commonplace materials. We used the surfaces as a generator of the architecture to make them operative, programmable, and functional.

With Tides, in New York, the seating and the kitchen were predetermined, but we found the space was taller than it was wide. The ceiling thus became fertile ground for architectural experimentation. In this case, we used thousands of bamboo skewers in the ceiling to create an inverted topography related to the morphology of tidal flows. This textured surrogate landscape is intended to combat the claustrophobia of the space and to direct visual attention upward, but it also acts as an acoustic and lighting filter, with fluorescent tubes suspended behind the acoustical foam tile. The constraint was specific, and we found an opportunity for creation and play. The restaurant Fluff, in New York, also evolved into a series of experiments with material, surface, and inexpensive, commonplace materials such as felt, which has a different resolution at a distance than from up close. In this case, we produced an interior "liner" for a bakery/café using approximately three linear miles of ¾-inch felt strips in varying shades of gray, stacked horizontally. This surface induced radically different optical effects based on the position of the viewer in the space and was intended to visually connect the store interior to the exterior and sidewalk. As in all the restaurant projects, we were also interested in optimizing the effect of a limited number of architectural components, so the "wrapper" also functions as a banquette, booth, acoustical dampening, and display surface.

NR These arrangements of simple materials as well as the repeated everyday stuff across the surface create a larger whole, losing a sense of their own physical material as they become a spatially activated surface: the voluminous massing of one hundred thousand skewers or felt strips. But another aspect of the restaurant projects you haven't touched on is that

you built them all by yourselves, something you were only able to do because of their small scale.

MT Our construction work came out of the pragmatism of getting things built with limited means in New York City. Our solutions are surprisingly simple: for instance, Fluff used masonry or tiling of the same modular size to produce complex effects. We have found there can be a lot of resistance within the construction industry to conditions which are not within standard practices or known means; so in many cases, to get the results we wanted, we had to take on certain aspects of these projects and build them ourselves. But with no construction standards, you have to think outside of conventional means, and as projects grow we can't continue to build them ourselves.

NR How then can projects move up a scale, both materially and spatially, and maintain the same criticality in terms of their relationship to the city? Perhaps the new scheme for the Arthouse, in Austin, Texas, exemplifies this in its use of glass block and the urban setting or the stone in the project.

MT I do think rather than repeating the same strategy with the small projects, there is an adaptive tactic, a capacity to move with agility between the restrictions to allow the specifics of the project to generate invention. The design for the Arthouse project is derived from the critical constraints, which in this case included the idiosyncrasies of the existing historic structure, which was initially a theater and then became a department store–both of which are by nature hermetically sealed spaces with little need for natural light or exchange with the exterior. Our work will open up the public nature of the institution with a street presence and increased permeability. However, within a limited budget, how do we strategically and selectively make surgical alterations to the existing envelope? One of the evident conditions is light. You don't want unfiltered daylight in a museum, but how do you control it? We introduced a series of laminated glass blocks, which would perforate the otherwise solid surface and allow for diffuse sunlight to filter into the buildings interior. We began with a regular grid and then migrated and aggregated the blocks relative to the programmatic requirements of the interior space. The building's program and structure was telegraphically mapped onto the public exterior. The blocks also play

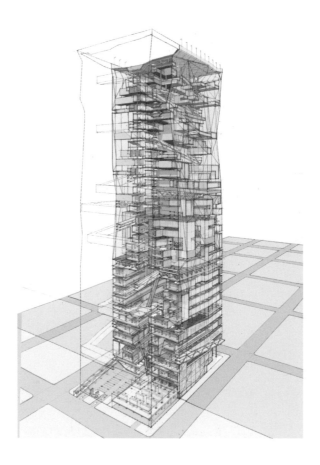

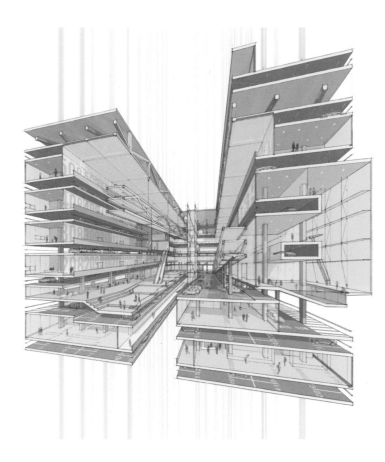

with shadow as they project through the wall in different depths. It is both adapting some of the strategies of the restaurants in patterning and surface but also a retranslation of these techniques to an urban and building scale.

NR How is cultural criticism played out in Arthouse?

MT The terms of the argument shift. With Arthouse, we are not attempting to erase the history of the building, but rather we are working with it as a context and a kind of palimpsest—at the same time questioning the idea of the white-box museum. For a contemporary *kunsthalle,* it is virtually impossible to predict the nature of the work displayed, and we felt the galleries should reflect their origins rather than pretend to neutrality. So the galleries became an active context rather than a passive backdrop. The interior walls are left as untreated rough masonry, the remnants of the theater and store are visible, and there is a flexible wall display system. It was also critical for us to challenge the boundaries between the institution and the city, thus the public is invited through the awning at the street level and drawn upward to a public roofscape. The threading through of the public into the institution will be a progressive one.

In the Park Tower project, we were dealing with a very different form of commission in which the charge from the curators was to address the typology of the parking garage in the context of an architectural exhibition. In this case the need to communicate through drawings and diagrams became part of the parameters of the project. On the other hand, we were interested in addressing the problem of parking in a precise way, beginning with certain metrics—the dimensional and circulation requirements of automobiles and the legislated relations between numbers of parking spaces and specified programs (hotel, shopping, office, residential, and so on)—and deriving the logic of the proposal from these prosaic constraints, albeit in an intentionally extreme and even absurdist way.

NR Apart from changes sponsored by shifts in scale, have there been alterations in methodology triggered by technological changes?

MT Yes. One of the ways we have been translating the ideas of repetition and complex patterning from the restaurant projects is through new techniques of fabrication. Whereas these earlier projects were, in a sense, very hands-on and material-intensive, we have been investigating ways to achieve similar effects though CNC milling and related technologies.

The new Memorial Sloane-Kettering Research Building, in New York City, designed by SOM, is an example of this—we were asked to design a sculptural installation for the main lobby space. The project engages notions of vision and motion inherent to this active entry space, making the act of looking itself the subject of the piece. The given here was a spatial volume within the lobby—a kind of thickened wall—which was intersected by a series of conical projections calibrated to a variety of visual trajectories within the lobby space. The intersection of these cones with the cubic volume of the wall produces a complex geometry of spatial and visual conditions that shift dynamically relative to the viewer's location in the space.

Because of the constructional logistics of the space and the requirements of manufacture, it was necessary to break the piece down into a series of 480 discrete cubes. These were laser-cut out of stainless steel and welded together for assembly on-site. The complex forms required digital control and study to attain the high level of precision required to fit each cube to another and produce the overall pattern. In the end it became the intersection with the conditions of fabrication that generated some of the most compelling aspects of the design.

NR You are also working on a project in a very exceptional context—culturally, climatically, and in terms of its specific client—in Inner Mongolia, as part of the Ordos 100 project. How did the peculiarities of this context drive the design?

MT We were dealing with not only an extreme climate in a literal sense but also the intense context of the Ordos project itself: one hundred villas, each designed by a different architect and constructed on a site at the edge of the Gobi Desert. We felt we had to respond to four primary factors: the local climate, the available technology, construction methods, and this highly unusual environment of—in some cases—radically different design approaches in close proximity to one another.

The design for the villa became a question of negotiating between the desire for exterior connections to the surrounding landscape and the

PREVIOUS PAGE Lewis.Tsurumaki.Lewis, Park Tower, installation at the American Pavilion, Venice Biennale, rendering, 2004.

LEFT Lewis.Tsurumaki.Lewis, Ordos House design, Inner Mongolia, rendering, 2009.

need to produce a sense of privacy and interiority for the inhabitants. The resulting form became an upper volume of private spaces and a public ground floor, which was characterized by a series of wrapping concrete walls. These walls extend from inside to outside and back in again to define a series of exterior courtyards directly related to the principal rooms of the villa. The courtyards set up a fluctuating relation between the inside and the outside, allowing for a relation to the intense sunlight and desert sky while preserving visual privacy and intimacy within this dense, exhibitionist environment. These walls also move up through the private spaces and carve out vertical voids to connect the two levels of the house.

Because of the limits of available construction techniques and materials, we tried to employ local materials for the primary components—for example, indigenous gray brick and concrete, which is made on-site— and restrict ourselves to forms that would be easy to execute using local construction techniques. However, while the wrapping walls are all consistently site-cast concrete on the exterior, they will be lined with warmer, richer materials internally—wood, tile, stone, etc.—to produce each as a unique space with contrasting qualities.

NR How did the principals in your firm come together from school to work on exhibition projects and then run projects all over the country?

MT Paul Lewis and I met at graduate school at Princeton, and upon graduation we both came to New York. I worked for Joel Sanders, and Paul worked for Diller + Scofidio. In spite of demanding schedules, we worked together on speculative projects and then exhibitions at the Storefront for Architecture and Artists Space. We were eventually joined by David Lewis. This partnership was the genesis of *Situation Normal,* which became a book in the Pamphlet Architecture series (Princeton Architectural Press, 1998). Later, we began getting commissions as a firm. We see our work as truly collaborative, even though the projects are getting larger. All three partners participate in the design of each project, especially in the earlier generative phases of the design. This redundancy is inefficient in a sense, but it does ensure each project is the result of an internal dialogue that hopefully makes the work stronger.

NR You all teach as well as practice. How does this challenge your ideas? How do you push your students to think critically about design?

MT I usually don't start a studio from a tabula rasa but from a real process of research and a close examination of conditions, which can be directed by the nature of the program. I do not assume everyone is operating in a vacuum. Thus, we often look at ordinary things—such as a standard hotel or the idiosyncracies of a given site—so that the students have materials to react to and against. The idea is not to replicate or repeat but to understand these strategies as a kind of cultural and ideological material to generate reinvention and response. This condition sets in motion a series of logics that can border on the absurd and can be unexpected but rational. As an architect, you have to justify your processes for the client as a set of logical steps, but you can twist those paths to operate in unexpected ways that can contradict the starting point. Students operate more efficiently if they have more to critique. My standpoint is that when they are successful, they take it seriously and derive an attitude and stance from something pre-existing. How do you get them to see something in an unbiased way? At Yale we looked at the specifics of a midscale building project that has very precise parameters in terms of site, program, and cultural content. The students were asked to engage the notion of limits at several scales, from that of the urban/landscape context to the specifics of the tectonic and material systems played out in detail.

NR I have been looking into the idea that architects by nature must be optimistic in order to create. Do you feel that way?

MT We all came out of an educational background that often relied upon a negative cultural critique. For us, the desire is not to use the critical to tear down but to posit something new and optimistic as a way of being propositional. It can introduce pleasure and play. This form of critique doesn't just pull something apart, but it can generate new conditions or possibilities. The aspiration is that one can operate in the realm of the critical and posit something productive and optimistic.

Amphibious Tactics

National parks, along with institutions like biological preserves, zoos, aquariums, and museums, are among the dominant sites in which ideas regarding the natural world are promulgated, disseminated, and received. While these spaces represent points of human access onto natural phenomena, they are also complex mechanisms of mediation and representation; as such, they can be seen as complicit in the construction of collective notions of the wild and humanity's place in nature. National parks may be the least obvious of these examples in that, on the surface, they would seem to simply preserve and protect large "wilderness" areas with a minimum of artifice. In fact, such parks constitute an assemblage of spatial practices that not only sequester large territories from their surrounding–rendering them distinct both in political status and in actual fact–but which also reconfigure, alter, and construct the landscapes they purport to preserve. In fact, the act of distinguishing these terrains from their surroundings inevitably transforms them, producing repercussions within larger regional and ecological systems. Paradoxically, these sites, which have in many ways come to represent the ideal of wilderness within the national imagination, are highly unnatural spaces, altered in fundamental ways to render them more meaningful and accessible in human terms.

LEFT Everglades National Park postcard, 1947. RIGHT Historic postcards of national parks.

This paradox is evident in the contradictory directives that launched the National Parks Service in 1916: "To conserve the scenery and to provide for the enjoyment of the same in such a manner and by such means as will leave them unimpaired for future generations." The mission of the Parks Service is to preserve, but to preserve primarily for human use and edification. Arising out of deeply held national beliefs regarding the salutary effects of exposure to nature, the emergence of the parks is imbricated within larger historical narratives regarding the shifting cultural value of the wilderness in the United States. While the institution of the National Parks Service marked an ideological and political sea change from a worldview in which nature was seen as an adversary to be overcome or exploited to one in which it became a source of edification and leisure, it remained primarily a human resource. This duplicity is transcribed in the inscription that marks the entry arch to Yellowstone National Park: FOR THE BENEFIT AND ENJOYMENT OF THE PEOPLE. In a variety of ways during the directive's ensuing 200-plus-year history, these contradictory impulses–between preservation and access, economic exploitation and scenic value, authentic experience and the necessity for human intervention–were played out in the landscapes, infrastructure, and architecture of the parks.

As one of the principal sources of our collective understanding of the wild, national parks intersect in compelling ways with the contemporary discourse regarding the human place *in* and impact *on* nature. As the global ecological situation is increasingly cast in terms of a crisis, ideas like sustainability, ecotourism, environmental ethics, biodiversity, and the like have come to prominence within the cultural and architectural debate. While these issues are endemic to architecture as such, operating in a protected territory such as a national park has the effect of intensifying the relationship between an architectural proposition and the precondition of its site, calling into question the conventional dialectic between building and landscape and provoking new potential interfaces between artificial and natural systems. Exploiting these possibilities, the investigations pursued within the fall 2006 Kahn studio sought to tease out the specific material parameters of one such space, Everglades National Park, as a source of limits, idiosyncrasies, contradictions, and paradox, generating architectural strategies derived from a close investigation of these given conditions. The intention here was not simply sustainability (though environmental questions were at play) nor strictly formal (though natural morphologies often served as a starting point) but rather the reinvention of any number of architectural commonplaces: programmatic (the typology of the lodge or resort), tectonic (techniques of enclosure, permeable membranes, structure/stability), and performative (the integration of both visual and environmental performance). In other words, the unique conditions of this volatile terrain were used as a catalyst to provoke new spatial potentials as well as to open up a broader discourse regarding how architecture collaborates in the construction of collective perceptions of the natural world.

NATIONAL PARKS: PRODUCING THE AMERICAN LANDSCAPE

The founding of the National Parks Service was a delayed response to the American conservation movement, which had its roots in the nineteenth-century anti-industrial impulses of European romanticism and the aesthetic ideals of the picturesque. Related equally to indigenous philosophical and artistic movements like transcendentalism and contemporary advances in scientific forestry, the origins of the conservation movement in America could be said to be an equal and opposite reaction to the fading of the frontier and the perceived loss of the "unspoiled" nature that it had represented: as described by historian Frederick Jackson Turner, the American encounter with the frontier—"the meeting point between savagery and civilization"—had served

LEFT Alligator Joe posing with a crocodile, ca. 1900. During the 1890s, William B. Frazee (a.k.a. Alligator Joe) ran the first alligator farms in West Palm Beach and Miami. RIGHT Cooper Town was a tourist attraction along Tamiami Trail. Cooper Town airboat, 1960s.

as a source of both individual (masculine) virtue and collective national character. The national parks played the role of both surrogate and memorial to the lost frontier. In this sense, the parks have always played both a pragmatic and symbolic role within public life.

LEFT National Audubon Society warden Charlie Brookfield leads a nature walk, 1947.
RIGHT Swamp buggy (Big Cypress), April 19, 1953.

From its inception, the conservation movement was embroiled in the conflict between scenic preservation (as embodied by naturalists like John Muir) and advocates of multiple use, as represented by the utilitarian agenda of the U.S. Forest Service (as personified by its first director, Gifford Pinchot). Whereas the preservationists wanted land to be safeguarded primarily for recreational use and the protection of scenic beauty, the conservationists advocated for the simultaneity of public access and commercial exploitation. Partly as a defense against the detrimental effects of "extractive industries" (logging, mining, grazing), tourism was put forth as an alternate generator of economic activity that would justify the preservation of wilderness in a virgin state. It was believed that tourism and nature tourism in particular "would create economic activity, prevent Americans from spending their money abroad, and inspire patriotic sentiments among an increasingly diverse population."[1] It was this shift from invasive industry to tourism as an economic engine that prefigured the rise of the Park Service in the early years of the twentieth century and which set in motion the conflicting agendas of preservation, public access, and profit that persist to this day.

With the emergence of tourism as "dignified exploitation" by the national parks, these wilderness areas increasingly came to be seen as commodified spaces for middle-class recreation. As the century progressed, these trends became more pronounced; as Christine Macy and Sarah Bonnemaisson write in *Architecture and Nature,* "In this context, nature was seen less as a lesson in civic virtue or a romantic reminder of the frontier, but as a modern space of leisure, as a space that was entertaining [and] safe."[2] Moreover, the evolution of the parks went hand in hand with the development of associated technological infrastructures, notably the national highway system. In fact, from its inception in the early part of the twentieth century to its apotheosis in the Eisenhower interstate network, the highway system is explicitly interrelated with the parks system: the highways stitched the national parks together into an interconnected matrix of regional landscapes that restructured the country at an unprecedented scale. In turn, the car domesticated and privatized the experience of nature, bringing with it the accoutrements of modern tourism: the family vacation, touring route, picnic site, and organized campground. In fact, the growth of "institutionalized forms of camping grew in conjunction with automotive access."[3] In combination with the predominance of the car, the vast increase in post–WW II attendance at the parks, sparked by economic expansion and a corresponding abundance of leisure time, meant these national preserves increasingly became the medium through which a generation of Americans came to form a cohesive image of the natural world.

[1] Ethan Carr, *Wilderness by Design: Landscape Architecture and the National Park Service.* University of Nebraska Press, 1998.

[2] Christine Macy and Sarah Bonnemaison, *Architecture and Nature: Creating the American Landscape.* London: Routledge: 2003.

[3] Ibid.

What is critical to consider here from the standpoint of architecture is not only how new infrastructures and technologies increased accessibility, but also how a complex repertoire of spatial and landscape techniques was brought to bear on the terrain of the parks, producing a massive restructuring of the perceptual apparatus through which these landscapes became apprehended by millions of visitors. Nature trails, scenic overlooks, parkways, photo opportunities, and the transformation of "natural attractions" into spatially coherent experiences were all part of the larger reorganization of the "'wild" into a controlled environment for touristic consumption. The visitors center, or interpretational facility—the emblematic structure of the wide-ranging Mission 66 initiative—clearly represents these tendencies. A hybrid of museum, service center, and administrative facility, the visitors center both literally and conceptually acts as the entry point to the park, establishing the terms by which the "authentic" phenomenon encountered within might be properly understood.

THE EVERGLADES: DOMESTICATING THE WILD

Nowhere are the paradoxes that characterize these spaces more evident than in the million and a half acres that constitute Everglades National Park, located on the southern tip of Florida. Perhaps more than any other American landscape, the Everglades embodies the intricate interplay between man-made and biotic systems, the ongoing push and pull between economics and conservation, and the fluidity of cultural values regarding the natural environment. Designated a World Heritage Site and an International Biosphere Reserve, the Everglades today represents one paradigm of the American wilderness for the million annual visitors that pass through its gates, although, well into the twentieth century, it had been considered an uninhabitable terrain with little intrinsic value. While home to a vast diversity of wildlife and plant species as well as several Native American communities, it was still largely unexplored by Europeans by the early 1900s, denigrated as a dangerous and pestilential swamp.

Seminole woman poling past billboard advertising sale of reclaimed land,
March 27, 1930. Probably Tamiami Canal.

Although seemingly vast as it exists today, the Everglades was originally far more extensive, a system of broad, shallow, and slow-moving rivers flowing from Lake Okeechobee in the north (near present-day Orlando) to Biscayne Bay in the south. The history of the ensuing one hundred years is one of continual human effort and intervention, ultimately resulting in the wholesale transformation of natural systems at a vast scale and with largely devastating results. While efforts to drain and domesticate the Everglades had been undertaken as early as 1880, dramatic population growth in the 1920s resulted in an increased human presence in the wetlands and devastating loss of life when Lake Okeechobee overflowed its levees in 1926 and again in 1928. Partially in response to these cataclysmic events, the U.S. Army Corps of Engineers undertook one of the largest water management projects in human history, establishing a massive system of levees, locks, and canals to control the unruly flows of the swamp and erecting the Herbert Hoover dike, which finally cut off the "river of grass" from its natural water source. While opening up vast tracts of land for agricultural use, these actions and subsequent development throughout the twentieth century continued to degrade the ecology of the Everglades, as more and more water was drawn off to feed the burgeoning coastal communities, resulting in drought, rampant fires, and disease among native animal populations. When the area was

Aerial photographs zooming in from general situation in Florida to the
water control station of the South New River Canal, in the Everglades.

finally dedicated as a national park in 1947, largely due to the efforts of individuals like conservationists Marjory Stoneman Douglass and Ernest F. Coe, much
of the damage had already been done, with the surviving, now-fragile ecosystem
a quarter of its original size and under continuing threats from desalinization,
the introduction of invasive species, encroaching development, and dramatic
changes to water chemistry wrought by agricultural toxins.

While subsequent efforts like the Comprehensive Everglades Restoration
Plan of 1998 have aspired to repair some of the damage of the last century, these
efforts ironically require ever-increasing degrees of technological intervention
to simulate conditions approximating the pre-Colonial hydrology of the park.
Today, the Everglades exists on infrastructural life support, both sustained
and threatened by human presence. Inside the park, there still exists the United
States' largest subtropical wilderness, which sponsors an astonishing degree
of biodiversity, while its borders are under continual pressure from the most
densely populated and fastest-developing region in the state. Under constant
renegotiation, the boundaries of the park represent a thin, unstable membrane
between a highly synthetic landscape and the fragile ecosystem within; but the
boundaries are also a striking illustration of how tenuous these distinctions have
become. As such, the Everglades represent an ideal site for a close examination
of architecture's relationship to biological, geological, and hydrological systems.

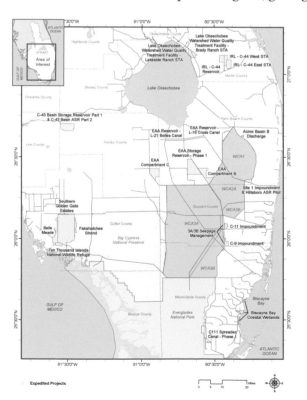

Map of the extent of water-control infrastructure in southern
Florida relating to the current hydrology of the Everglades.

METHODOLOGY: EXPLOITING LIMITS

The tensions that characterize the history of the national parks in general and the Everglades in particular—tensions between conservation and access, artifice and the desire for authentic experience, the preservation of biological diversity and the legitimacy of human use—underscore the shifting nature of our collective attitude and perception regarding the natural environment. Today, a whole new range of practices and concepts have emerged, from sustainability to eco-tourism, which require a wholesale reconsideration of how the built environment might engage the question of the so-called natural. While architects and our professional and academic institutions have gradually come to recognize the critical status of such questions, too often the bureaucratic response has been to place them within a predetermined framework of formulaic solutions applied to conventional forms and systems. The Yale studio sought to address the question of how a higher degree of environmental intelligence might sponsor not only more ecologically viable buildings, but also more imaginative architectural formations. Rather than take the moralistic obligations of sustainability as a negative burden to be fulfilled, the approach of the studio was to see these imperatives as positive generators of architectural form. The studio asked how such practices might sponsor a radical reconsideration of how a building operates, suggesting a performative basis for an architecture that engages natural processes and organic systems not as stylistic appliqué or in terms of formal mimesis but as a part of the functional logic of the proposal.

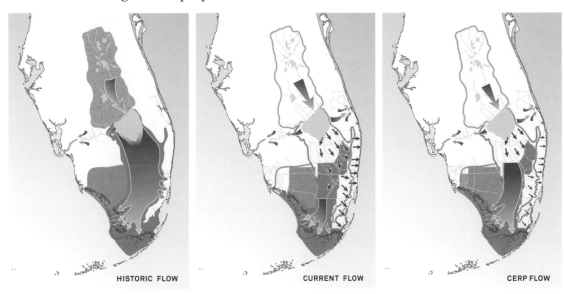

Comparative diagrams showing proposed "restoration" of historical flow under the 1998 Comprehensive Everglades Restoration Plan (CERP).

Mining the rich contemporary debate surrounding the ecological and the architectural as source material, the investigations conducted within the studio sought to examine how the highly charged context of a protected territory like the Everglades could sponsor architectural strategies derived from a close investigation of the unique landscape of the park. Operating in the volatile and semifluid terrain of the Everglades—where distinctions between land and water are blurred and in which minor variations in elevation result in radical transformations in landscape—required a rethinking of commonplace notions of enclosure, materiality, program, stability, and performance. Students were encouraged to develop a set of architectural tactics related to the precise parameters and limits presented by the site, often attaching themselves to representative landscape conditions, the qualities of which served as a catalyst for rethinking the terms of the problem in each case. The contention of the studio was that the simultaneity of technical, architectural, and biotic systems has the potential to generate unprecedented formal and material solutions, which must be nevertheless strictly rational on their own terms. By amplifying the operational demands of the building, the project sought a multivalent architecture that operated at a diversity of levels, engendering productive overlaps between form, space, technologies, and program.

Refusing an easy delineation between natural and artificial systems, these projects also resisted the notion of their unproblematic synthesis or symbiosis. The given program, a lodge (which exists typologically between a campground and hotel/motel), assumed the possibility of longer-term human inhabitation and therefore implied a substantial intervention as well as an unavoidable presence in the landscape of the park (buried buildings are not physically possible in the Everglades). In many cases, the proposals either intentionally acted as a parallel or surrogate for landscape or attached themselves to larger infrastructures involved in the operation of the parks: transportation networks, water management technology, and so on. In other instances, the projects sought to provide a kind of register or datum against which the shifting qualities of landscape could be amplified. Celebrating the confluence of natural and man-made systems at play, the projects looked for opportunities to exploit the paradoxes of their coexistence.

Ultimately, the studio sought to navigate the difficult territory between architecture and environment, between the constructed and the "natural." Critical to this examination was a recognition of the complex entanglement of these terms. At a moment when the distinctions between the natural and the artificial have become problematized within theoretical discourse, the man-made and organic systems that collectively comprise the physical environment are becoming increasingly difficult to disentangle. The "natural" world is in a double sense culturally constructed: both materially (through the effects of technological and infrastructural organizations) and conceptually (through a multiplicity of discourses—scientific, philosophical, political). The studio attempted to go beyond these inherited distinctions, with an emphasis on how issues of sustainability can become a stimulus for rethinking the conventional relationship between architecture and landscape.

Marc Tsurumaki

BIBLIOGRAPHY

Bachelard, Gaston, *Water and Dreams: An Essay on the Imagination of Matter,* Dallas: The Pegasus Foundation, 1983.

Carr, Archie, *The Everglades,* New York: Time-Life Books, 1973.

Cronon, William. ed., *Uncommon Ground: Toward Reinventing Nature,* New York: W. W. Norton & Co., 1995.

Davis, Steven and Ogden, John C., eds., *The Everglades: The Ecosystem and Its Restoration,* Boca Raton: St. Lucie Press, 1994.

Douglas, Marjory Stoneman, *The Everglades: River of Grass* (1947), Sarasota: Pineapple Press, 1997.

Haraway, Donna J. Simians, *Cyborgs and Women: The Reinvention of Nature,* New York: Routledge, 1991.

Grunwald, Michael, *The Swamp, the Everglades, Florida, and the Politics of Paradise.* New York: Simon & Schuster, 2006.

Lejeune, Jean Francois and Schulman, Alan T., *The Making of Miami Beach: 1933-42,* New York: Rizzoli, 2000.

Lodge, Thomas, *The Everglades Handbook: Understanding the Ecosystem,* Boca Raton: CRC Press, 2004.

McCally, David, *The Everglades: An Environmental History,* Gainesville: University Press of Florida, 1999.

McClellan, Linda Flint, *Building the National Parks: Historic Landscape Design and Construction,* Baltimore: Johns Hopkins University Press, 1998.

Ockman, Joan and Frausto, Salomon, *Architourism: Authentic, Escapist, Exotic, Spectacular,* New York: Prestel Press, 2006.

Luke, Timothy W., *Ecocritique: Contesting the Politics of Nature, Economy, and Culture,* Minneapolis: University of Minnesota Press, 1997.

Wilson, Alexander. *The Culture of Nature: North American Landscape from Disney to the Exxon Valdez,* Cambridge: Blackwell, 1992.

Park Lodge / Resort

INTRODUCTION

The studio operated through an exploitation of limits, examining the manner in which constraints can provide the catalyst for architectural invention. Such a methodology entails an imaginative engagement with restrictions—a renegotiation of the complex network of use values, political imperatives, technological systems, consumer desires, site parameters, and economic formulas, all of which invariably circumscribe the architectural project. By maneuvering tactically among these operational boundaries, the latencies of normative configurations can be teased out, generating new spatial and material possibilities from within the logics of the given. In this way, architectural production is recast as a form of restricted play, a pleasurable manipulation of bounds and constraints. Prerequisite to this approach is a relentless curiosity, in the sense expounded by Michel Foucault—a "readiness to find strange and singular what surrounds us; a certain relentlessness to break up our familiarities and to regard otherwise the same things; a fervor to grasp what is happening and what passes; a casualness in regard to the traditional hierarchies of the important and the essential."[4]

Shark Valley Observation Tower ramp, an example of an extant parks-service structure.

More specifically, the studio examined the way in which extreme political and physical limits can catalyze the architectural imagination through the juxtaposition of a "normative" program with an extraordinary site condition. Examining the collision of nature tourism with the protected territory of a national park, the studio interrogated the relationship between conflicting desires for access to the wild (nature as a site of recreation and tourism) and the demands of a volatile ecosystem (nature as preserve). The project comprises a new resort lodge within the boundaries of Everglades National Park to replace existing facilities damaged in the recent hurricanes. The volatile nature of the site, both in terms of its protected status and its material ambiguity, demanded the architectural negotiation of several apparently contradictory constraints.

Primary among these is the shifting and unstable landscape of the Everglades itself. The quasi-aquatic conditions of this liquid terrain requires the invention of amphibious architectures which take as their site the flows and accumulations of the glades. While most architectures must engage water at the most prosaic level—weatherproofing, humidity regulation, plumbing, and so on—this project proposes an imaginative rethinking of the intersection between architecture and water. This paradoxical coupling of apparently contradictory entities—water is seen as fluid and dynamic, architecture as static and fixed—became the catalyst for speculation. Analogous to the often bizarre-seeming adaptations of biological

4 Foucault, Michel, "The Masked Philosopher" in *Foucault Live: (Interviews, 1961–1984)*, trans. John Johnson (New York: Semitexte) Double Agent Series, 1996, 196–99.

organisms to extreme environmental conditions, inhabitation of such an insecure milieu required of the students invention, agility, and a radical rethinking of commonplace notions of stability, permanence, structure, ground, and enclosure.

Further, the studio considered the ways in which tourism and leisure practices impact and shape the natural environment as well as the conflicting agendas that coalesce in spaces like nature preserves and the national parks. Our national parks remain one of the principal sites in which ideas—such as human and animal, nature and culture, city and wilderness—are produced, negotiated, and consumed. However, at a time when the stability of these categories has been progressively eroded and our relationship to the global environment has been cast in terms of crisis, the park as an institution increasingly has become a site of conflicting desires and competing agendas as well as a nexus in which economy and ecology, touristic desires and conservationist ethics coexist. Navigating emergent terms such as *eco-tourism* and *sustainability,* we engaged the multiple ways in which economic, cultural, and material practices come together in the formation of landscape, exploiting the contradictions found to provoke new spatial, material, and programmatic possibilities.

LIMIT ONE : SITE

Swamp
While universally perceived now as an indispensable national and natural resource, the vast riparian ecosystem known as the Everglades was once unanimously decried as a "vast and useless marsh," a "God-forsaken wilderness suitable only for noxious vermin" and "pestilential reptiles." Neither land nor water, the Everglades is in reality not so much a swamp as an extremely slow-moving and shallow river, a horizontal flow of water through sawgrass and a staggering diversity of life. Once covering the majority of what is now south Florida, from present-day Orlando to the Florida Keys, the Everglades has undergone a series of radical transformations, both in terms of its physical form as well as its position within the popular imagination. Perhaps more than any other place, the Everglades epitomizes the shifting nature of material, the fluidity of values, and the varying substance of our ideas regarding the natural world.

As recently as 1897, the Everglades remained a terra incognita. According to one contemporary explorer, it was "as much unknown to the white man as the heart of Africa." Considered uninhabitable for decades and resistant to attempts at domestication, the "swamp" eventually ceded under the assault of the Army Corps of Engineers in the form of one of the largest water management projects ever attempted, initiated in response to a deadly 1928 hurricane that killed 2,500 people. A massive infrastructural undertaking that altered the flows and patterns of a vast territory, the so-called Central and Southern Florida Project installed a matrix of dams, levees, and canals intended to manage the unmanageable and render the unruly bog a productive landscape. While a boon to the agribusiness pioneers who turned the newly drained land into an extensive network of sugarcane farms, the project essentially cut off the Everglades from its natural source of water, resulting in an ecological morass that persists to this day. These and subsequent efforts to tame the Everglades effectively reduced its expanse by half and wreaked havoc on the remaining area in the form of drought, fire, and disease. The area became "protected" as a national park in 1947.

Today, the area once occupied by the Everglades ecosystem has been transformed into a dense play land with millions of residents and tourists. Less than an hour from the tourist enclaves of Miami Beach, the park is under continual pressure from the rapid development of southern Florida. The borders of the Everglades have become a virtual battlefield where economic interests and environmental politics meet and where an ever-expanding carpet of mini-mansions, biotech campuses, and big-box stores edges farther into the wetlands on a daily basis. Simultaneously, recent attempts to rectify the damage done earlier in the century, like the CERP (Comprehensive Everglades Restoration Plan) proposal of 1998, have resulted in more interventions into this contested landscape in the interest of returning it to its pre-Colonial state—a condition which, paradoxically, can now only be simulated through a complex assembly of technological and infrastructural systems. In the Everglades, conventional distinctions between the natural and the artificial are no longer possible or even operationally significant.

LIMIT TWO : PROGRAM

Resort

The program addressed the competing desires in the form of a park-sponsored hotel or lodge. Lodgings in national parks have historically ranged from rustic campsites to grand hotels (like the inns at Yellowstone or the Grand Canyon), which incorporated the most urbane accommodations. Combining domestic comfort with a proximity to scenic wilderness sites, these buildings represented a particular subset of the hotel typology: the architectural features were calibrated to satisfy visitors' fantasies of escape and isolation while providing a level of amenity and even luxury appropriate to the newly affluent leisure class. Linked to the rise of rail and early automotive tourism, these lodges embodied emerging contradictions within the collective national perception of the wild.

Today, the management of lodgings and hotels within the parks is largely in the hands of private companies like Xanterra Resorts, which until recently operated the Flamingo Lodge at Everglades National Park. Essentially a hundred-room resort hotel and marina situated at the eastern edge of the park; the lodge remains inoperable due to damage sustained in past hurricanes. The project assumed the relative scale and function of this facility while allowing for the possibility of a new site (or sites) for the proposed intervention.

While tied into longer narratives of nature-based tourism, leisure, and recreation, visitation to national parks like the Everglades intersects in an obvious way with the growing popularity of eco-tourism and a renewed interest in the environment. In fact, eco-tourism is the most rapidly growing sector of the tourism industry, constituting a distinctly twenty-first century mutation of twentieth-century touristic practices. If conventional tourism entails a mediated relation to place—a system of technological and ideological filters that reify, reduce, and commodify the complexity of place—then in nature tourism, the alterity of the foreign is replaced by the authenticity of the wild. Appealing to the desire for a transparent experience of the non-human, eco-tourism attempts to play mass tourism against itself, striking a delicate balance between development and preservation. The studio engaged the logics of these cultural practices, exploiting their latent contradictions to rethink the permeable boundaries between the constructed and the natural.

Method

The studio operated through the amplification of the latencies and potentials of normative programmatic and tectonic configurations. Rather than an externally generated formal strategy to be retroactively programmed, we sought new architectural tactics that operate opportunistically and playfully from within the logics and limits of given systems and parameters. Through an examination and subsequent manipulation of the social and spatial protocols at hand, we attempted to critically renegotiate the terms of engagement between bodies, landscapes, and technologies—resulting in projects that engaged the themes of Infrastructural Terrains, Surrogate Natures, and Datum, as the students explored new terrains of possibilities.

BELOW Everglades habitat section (Jeff McBride).

1. Infrastructural Terrains

The theme Infrastructural Terrains encompasses investigations in which an infrastructural condition serves as the framework for the formation of an architectural proposition. These architectures accrete around, derive from, or otherwise inhabit infrastructural systems such as hydrological and transportation networks (cars, roads), extending their logics and organizations to generate new spatial and programmatic conditions.

1.A
Allen Slamic

This project provides for lodging, recreation, canoeing, and hiking in the Florida Everglades. The specific design proposes a new series of trails and roadways to connect to a larger network throughout the central and northern sections of Everglades National Park. The chosen site is the sawgrass marshes at Pa-Hay Okee Overlook. The design uses the existing Pa-Hay Okee Overlook parking lot for new stack parking and an elevated RV campground, as well as an elevated scenic loop road for vehicular travel and observation. Due to the high dependency of the park on cars, infrastructure that integrates the automobile, RVs, and campers becomes vital for full engagement of the surrounding environments.

The lodging strategy turns to single prefabricated units, which are dispersed throughout the sawgrass marsh in close proximity to the parking structure. With the tactically positioned units, a variety of private and public relationships are formed along the interstitial spaces between each unit. An armature for vine growth encourages an optimal and natural shading device from the hot south Florida climate; the trellis structure not only controls the density and distribution of plant growth but also works as the structural frame network for harnessing the lodges and circulation paths as it weaves and takes shape around the aggressive vegetation of the Everglades.

The south Florida region offers a large number of native vines in a variety of colors, from the Coral Honeysuckle to the Key Morning Glory. With the vines placed around the structural armature in random clusters and some patterns, the seasonal flowering creates a shifting color spectrum throughout the project as the seasons unfold, thus transforming architecture through nature. The close interaction between architecture and nature begins to blur the edge between man-made and natural environments.

With the integration of the parking infrastructure, the prefabricated lodges, and an efficient structural system, this architecture differentiates between spatial conditions and social relationships while enhancing their relationship with the distinctive landscape of the Everglades that has not existed previously.

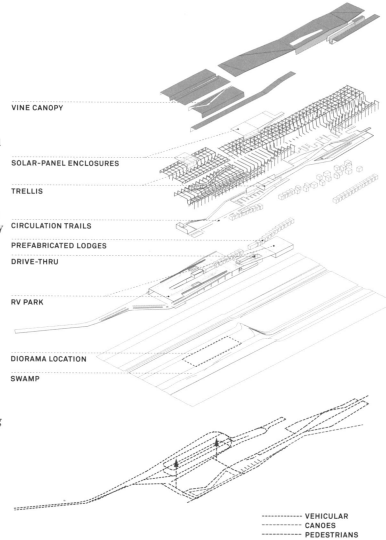

VINE CANOPY

SOLAR-PANEL ENCLOSURES

TRELLIS

CIRCULATION TRAILS

PREFABRICATED LODGES

DRIVE-THRU

RV PARK

DIORAMA LOCATION

SWAMP

------------ VEHICULAR
------------ CANOES
------------ PEDESTRIANS

1.A.1

1.A.1
Site strategy diagram
axonometric.

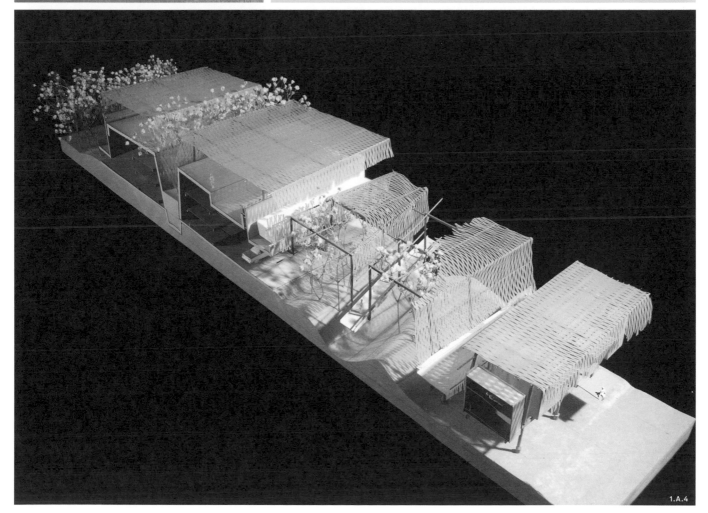

1.A.2
Perspective through
landscape.

1.A.3
Preliminary perspective
from elevated RV park
looking out toward
the typical Everglades
landscape.

1.A.4
Overall aerial view
of sectional model.

EXISTING PARK CIRCULATION

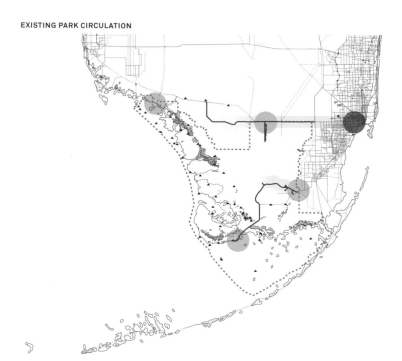

PROPOSED PARK CIRCULATION

PROPOSED SITE - - - - - - - - - - - -

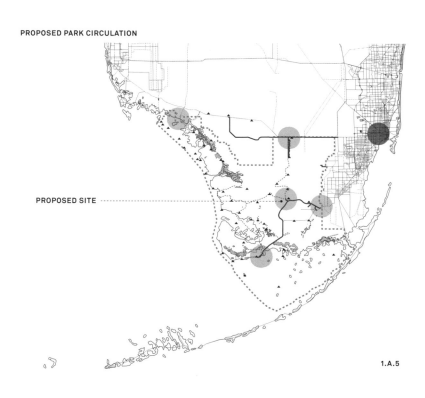

1.A.5

CONE OF VISION FROM PARK ROADS
▲   CAMPING LOCATIONS
    MAIN VISITORS CENTERS
    MIAMI
- - - - - -   CANOE TRAILS
————————   PARK ROADS
- - - - - - -   PARK BOUNDARIES

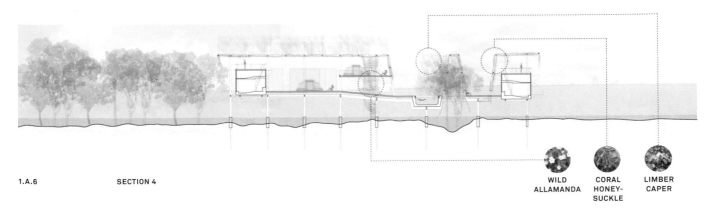

1.A.6   SECTION 4

WILD
ALLAMANDA

CORAL
HONEY-
SUCKLE

LIMBER
CAPER

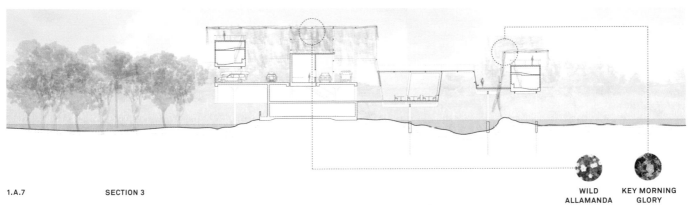

1.A.7   SECTION 3

WILD
ALLAMANDA

KEY MORNING
GLORY

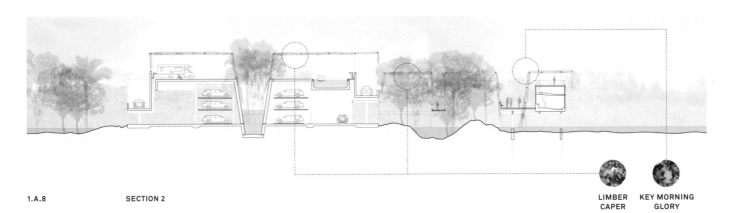

1.A.8   SECTION 2

LIMBER
CAPER

KEY MORNING
GLORY

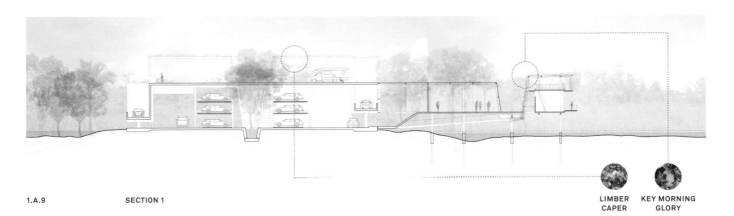

1.A.9   SECTION 1

LIMBER
CAPER

KEY MORNING
GLORY

1.A.5
Existing and proposed
site circulatory dia-
grams.

1.A.6
First section through
RV parking structure
and lobby.

1.A.7
Second section through
RV parking structure
and prefabricated lodg-
ing units.

1.A.8
Third section through
prefabricated lodging
units and drive-through
restaurant.

1.A.9
Fourth section through
communal living area
and swimming pool.

1.B
Adrienne E. Swiatocha

Research on the pressures of urban development on the Ever-glades revealed the extent to which the political boundaries out-side the park have had drastic physical manifestations inside the park. This project, "Slough Lodge," investigates the possibility of urban development and natural systems to not only coexist but also enhance the experience and performance of one an-other. The project situates itself on the northern Tamiami Trail (Route 41), the northern boundary edge of the park, and its islandlike configuration allows water, flora, and fauna to pass through it and into the park. The shape of the section captures light and water and harvests wind for passive climatic control. Terracing and view moments allow for seasonal changes to be measured and emphasized.

Sites
The existing Flamingo Lodge that was destroyed in 2005 by Hurricanes Katrina and Wilma is sited at the southernmost tip of Everglades National Park. This location required visitors to drive approximately forty minutes through the park itself to reach the lodge; it also required vast human intervention such as service roads and utilities to be imposed on this fragile environment. From Miami at the east and Naples at the west, the park is accessed by Route 41, the so-called Tamiami Trail, a road that also forms its northern edge and runs perpendicular to the flow of the slough, the wide, slow-moving shallow river that characterizes the Everglades as home to so many unique organisms. A few large canals have been built to allow the passage of water from its source, Lake Okeechobee, to the park but have also altered its direction and rate of flow. Over time this has caused a dramatic change in the landscape. Airboat traffic for tourism has also carved channels through the land-scape that alter the flow of the slough. Satellite images reveal that miniature land formations called tree islands have been dramatically re-formed over time.

The new lodge, sited at this road, allows visitors direct access to the unique landscape of the Everglades while giving the preserve the space and time it needs to rebound from the environmental degradation that has put these natural species so close to extinction. The existing lodge is sited on dry land outside of the boundaries of the slough, even during the wettest months. The new lodge is completely embedded in the heart of the slough, immersing the visitor in the experience. The massing and form of the lodge itself acts to redirect the flow of water to reproduce its historical flow patterns and restore the immediate area to natural conditions.

Programming/Organization
The proposed Slough Lodge comprises three main elements: sawgrass terracing, concrete islands, and sleeping units above. The nine interconnected island formations allow water to flow through the lodge and provide plinths for social programming, such as swimming pools, a restaurant, lounge, museum, and tourist administration offices. Exterior terraces transition from plinth to channel, and subtle elevational changes allow the rise and fall of water levels—wet summers, dry winters—to be visually amplified throughout the year. The sculpted terraces also support miniaturized versions of Everglades ecosystems for viewing in a setting that becomes internalized into the lodge footprint; because ecosystems in the Everglades are differenti-ated by elevation, each ecosystems is represented in this one accessible area. The sleeping units above the social program are organized around shared outdoor "living rooms," which are contained on one side by an organic wall positioned to absorb sunlight and use captured rainwater so that it may support local Everglades flora year-round. This "living wall" attracts Everglades birds and other wildlife to feed, nest, and otherwise display themselves to the guest in an intimate environment. The section of the sleeping units is shaped for optimal shading in the summer and light penetration during the winter months. The living wall acts as a visual backdrop for all spaces public and private but also gives privacy to the sleeping units. Water harvested during the hot and humid summer months trickles down and temporarily converts the living wall to a radiant cooling surface. Combining low wall-air-intake penetration with exhaust penetrations as high as thirty feet allows for stack-effect passive ventilation to cool off visitors in the hot summer months.

The lodge serves as a teaching tool, not only to learn about the unique characteristics of the Florida Everglades but also as an example of how human development and the act of protecting and restoring nature are not mutually exclusive. The building acts as a living, breathing organism, and like all other organisms serves to benefit the greater system of living things. The intimate connection made between the visitor and this complex environment is meant to promote and encourage stewardship of one's own environment.

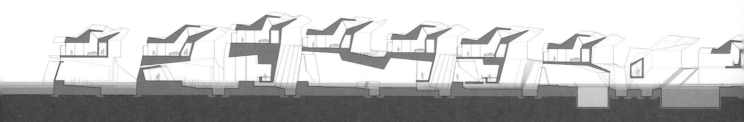

1.B.1

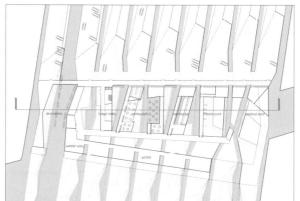

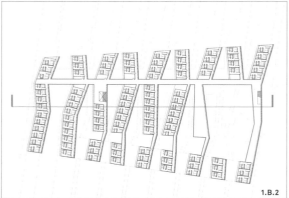

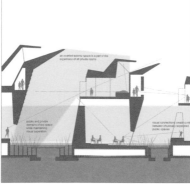

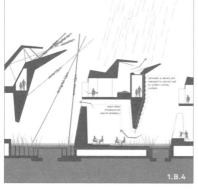

1.B.1
Longitudinal section.

1.B.2
Bird's-eye view from
southeast.

1.B.3
Section through the
lodge facing south, with
views into both public
and private spaces and
indoor and outdoor
programs.

1.B.4
Environmental and
experiential diagrams:
the perfomative section
serves to environmen-
tally condition the spaces
and create segregation
between public and
private while maintaining
connection to wildlife.

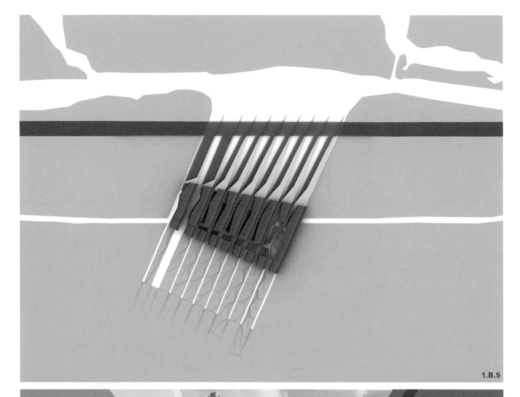

1.B.5

1.B.6

1.B.5
Site plan showing rela-
tionship of building site
to the Tamiami Trail.
Slough water is allowed
to penetrate the building
at multiple points to
restore flow rate, direc-
tion, and depth.

1.B.6
Internalized, outdoor
shared "living rooms"
allow an intimate con-
nection to Everglades
wildlife.

1.C
Anya A. Grant

In 2005, Hurricanes Katrina and Wilma struck the southern coast of Florida, destroying the Flamingo Lodge, the only accommodation located within the Everglades National Park. The lodge was subsequently closed.

To undertake the project of rebuilding, one must acknowledge the challenges of this unique site and respond with a suitably robust architecture. However, the susceptibility of the fragile ecosystem to prevalent development pressures also requires a resort in the Everglades be unobtrusive. Rather than rebuild the cabins, motel rooms, and campground areas lost to the hurricane on the flood-prone site, this project seeks to respond to the aquatic environment with a resort that at once thematizes the river and treats it responsibly. The infrastructure of existing water-flow management systems provides a model for the construction of a responsible development in which environmental remediation and ecotourism can coexist.

With concern for the preservation of water quality, the state of Florida has produced Stormwater Treatment Areas (STAs) to the north of the park. These are surface-treatment wetlands in which levees are used to define parallel beds of remediative plant species that exploit the natural direction of water flow through them to purify the runoff from agricultural land. Additionally, the Tamiami Levee, located just north of the Everglades National Park, acts as a buffer, slowing the entry of runoff from agricultural lands into the federally protected park. A proposal is under way to demolish the levee in order to restore the overall southward flow of water through the parched Everglades, which action would also increase the flow of agricultural runoff into the protected waters of the park. This project proposes that, instead of demolishing the levee, a level of porosity that mimics the STAs could mediate the flow of pollutants into the controlled waters of the park while also framing recreational water use.

To minimize the impact of new construction, the resort attaches itself to the south side of the Tamiami Levee, which carries the major east-west highway, U.S. Route 41, through the Everglades. The wetlands are effectively an extension of the highway surface—three asphalt-lined beds aligned parallel to the levee, which also collect runoff from the road surface. To reinstate flow across the buffer zone, culverts through the levee and the resort align the local water system to the natural flow of the Everglades. In the wet season, when the culverts are full, water overflows into the treatment wetlands and is treated locally before being released into the National Park. Within the treatment beds and among the remediative plants, extended concrete plinths provide the hidden superstructure that supports the hotel rooms. Guest rooms seem to float among the native species and are arrayed around the wetlands to enclose opportunities for recreational activities, such as fishing and bird watching. In the drier periods, the busy tourist season in the Everglades, gray water produced by guests' daily hotel rituals is channeled into the treatment wetlands before reentering the Everglades, thus creating an oasis for plant and animal life.

The flow of water through the room in narrow channels is coordinated with the ritual of the guests' activities. Contiguous paths through the bedroom and bathroom follow the domestic activities of grooming and sleeping. These paths are directed to allow the room's plumbing to feed into the larger phytoremediative system. Each room is equipped with a settling pond that pre-treats the gray water produced within before releasing it into the treatment wetlands. The vegetation supporting the settling pond is sufficiently high to provide a privacy screen for the largely open room. In addition to the visual and physical connections to the outside, the plumbing of the individual rooms is integrally tied to the wetlands. As a luxury alternative to camping in the Everglades, the lodge manages to maintain a significant connection with its distinctive setting.

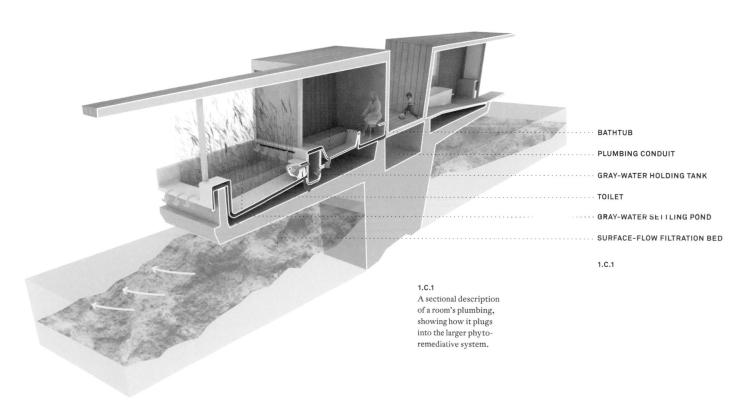

BATHTUB

PLUMBING CONDUIT

GRAY-WATER HOLDING TANK

TOILET

GRAY-WATER SETTLING POND

SURFACE-FLOW FILTRATION BED

1.C.1

1.C.1
A sectional description of a room's plumbing, showing how it plugs into the larger phytoremediative system.

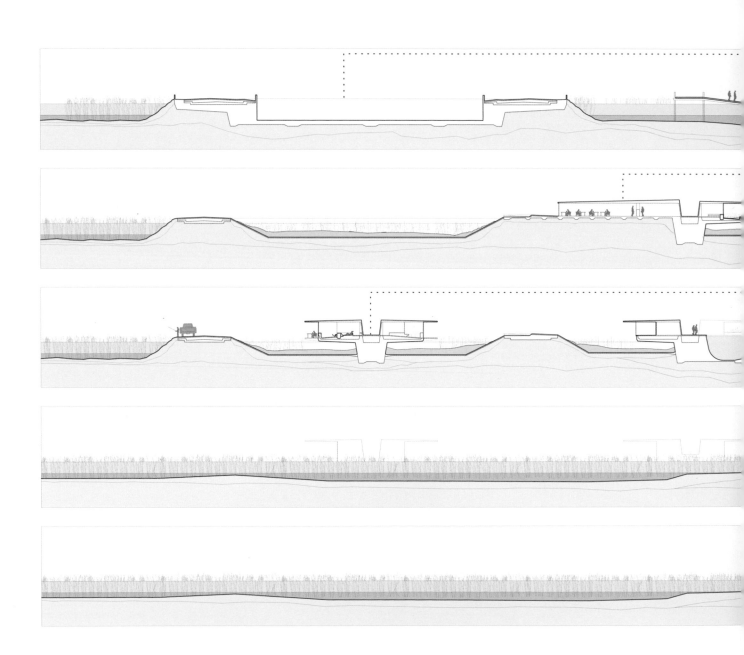

1.C.2
The evolution of the
room layout, which
seeks to align guests'
daily grooming rituals
along a path that mim-
ics the flow of water
through the room's
plumbing.

1.C.3
The levee system is
expanded and special-
ized to accommodate
recreation and
remediation.

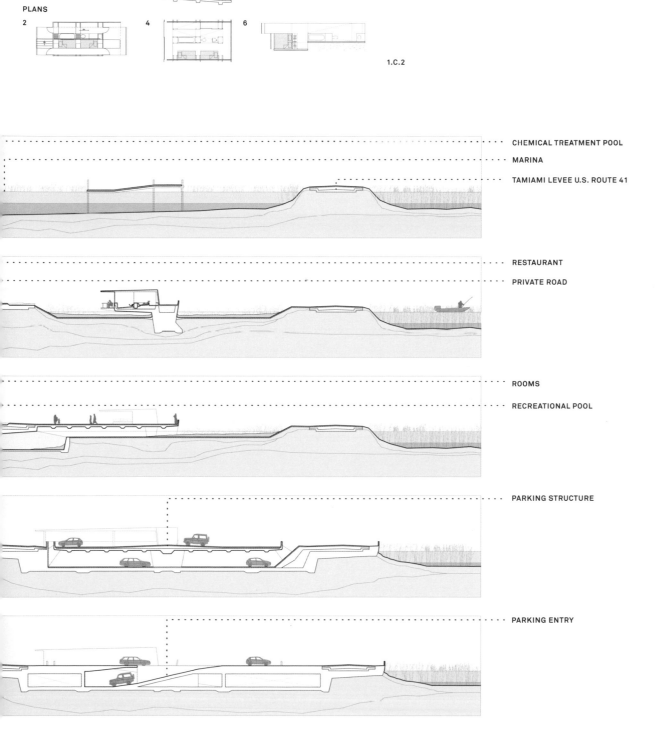

SECTIONS

1 3 5

PLANS

2 4 6

1.C.2

CHEMICAL TREATMENT POOL
MARINA
TAMIAMI LEVEE U.S. ROUTE 41

RESTAURANT
PRIVATE ROAD

ROOMS
RECREATIONAL POOL

PARKING STRUCTURE

PARKING ENTRY

1.C.3

1.D
Geoffrey Lawson

The purpose of this project is threefold: to design a new lodge and campground for Everglades National Park to replace the existing facility destroyed during Hurricanes Katrina and Rita while considering how one should inhabit a national park; to create a place of dwelling that doubles as a gray-water recycling facility and institute for sustainable water usage; and to challenge the traditional separation of architecture and landscape architecture to allow for the potential of new typologies.

The resulting scheme condenses all the programmatic requirements into a single urban environment suited for walking and social encounters while reducing the overall amount of disturbed territory occupied by the complex. The main bulk of the building is placed over an existing parking lot at the point of convergence of existing automobile, bus, boating, and hiking infrastructures and thus emerges as a node of hybridized activity.

At a macro scale, the complex orients itself to take advantage of sweeping views over the vast horizontal landscape and enforces the natural boundary between a brackish coastal prairie dotted with mangrove forests and the freshwater marine environment of Florida Bay. While defining and enhancing the specific microclimatic conditions of these zones, this strategy also knits together discrete landscapes by re-creating the natural flow of water, which was disrupted with the construction of the existing parking lots and roads, through the creation of an artificial tidal estuary.

At a micro scale, the synthetic estuary, made through the use of hanging mangrove gardens, spatializes the Everglades experience and forms a habitable landscape for camping that overlooks Florida Bay to the south. Likewise, the ramped viewing platform embeds a network of multifunctional terraced hotel suites perched over the mangrove forests. Akin to tree houses, these rooms mimic the lagoonlike nature of the mangroves and emit diffused light from the north.

The form of the Z-shaped ramp was chosen for its ability to emerge from and integrate with the ground while also taking on a strong figural iconicity. It is performative in the processes of water treatment, allowing for the directional flow of water while also fluctuating the speed of that flow at regular intervals, thus allowing for the filtering of contaminents and the removal of silt.

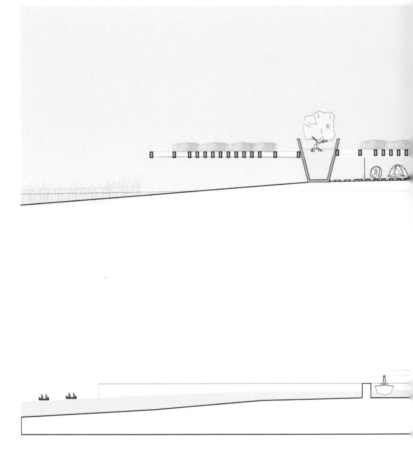

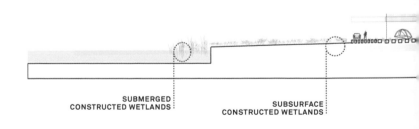

SUBMERGED
CONSTRUCTED WETLANDS

SUBSURFACE
CONSTRUCTED WETLANDS

1.D.1
Sectional perspective.

1.D.2
Site section.

1.D.3
Site section.

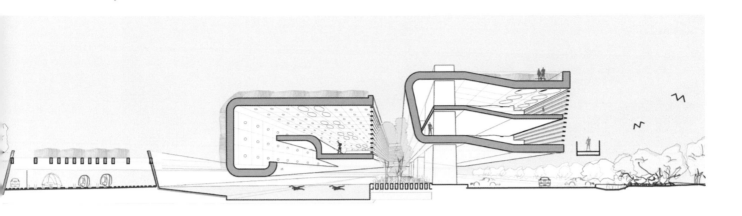

1.D.1

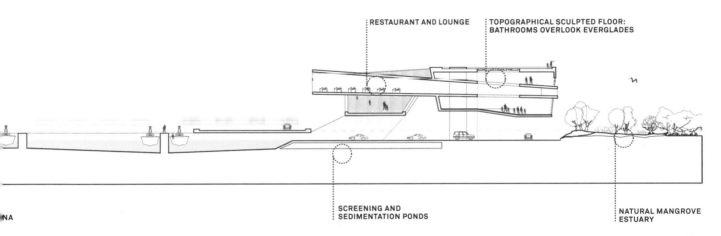

RESTAURANT AND LOUNGE   TOPOGRAPHICAL SCULPTED FLOOR:
BATHROOMS OVERLOOK EVERGLADES

NA

SCREENING AND
SEDIMENTATION PONDS

NATURAL MANGROVE
ESTUARY

1.D.2

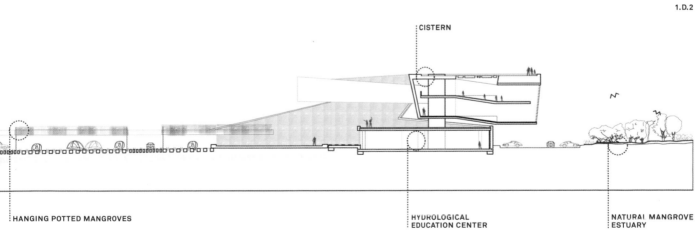

CISTERN

HANGING POTTED MANGROVES

HYDROLOGICAL
EDUCATION CENTER

NATURAL MANGROVE
ESTUARY

1.D.3

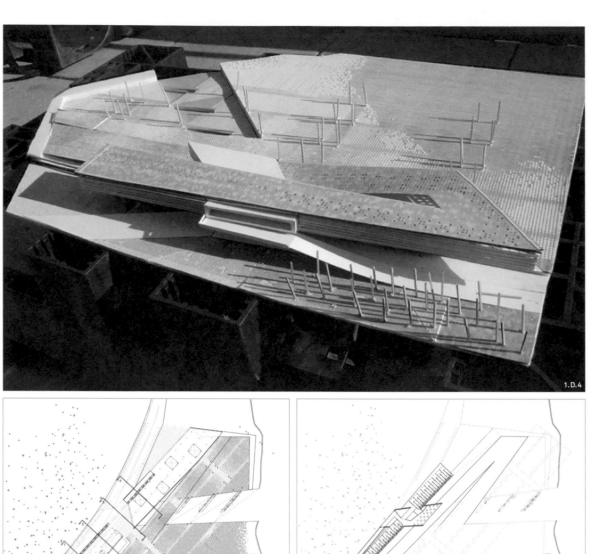

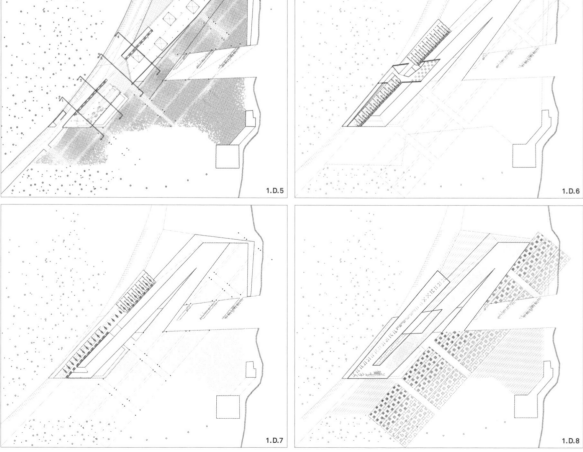

1.D.4
Aerial view of model.

1.D.5
First floor plan:
education and
recreation program

1.D.6
Second floor plan:
utility and communal
program.

1.D.7
Third floor plan:
habitation program.

1.D.8
Roof plan: vegetation
program.

2. Surrogate Nature

The theme, Surrogate Nature, focuses on projects in which the architectural proposition in terms of scale, performative characteristics, or perceptual effects operates as a form of "second nature." These projects embrace the artificiality of the intervention while at the same time referencing and intensifying natural phenomenon, intentionally obfuscating the lines between the constructed and the natural.

2.A

Gabrielle Brainard

This hotel and spa for Everglades National Park is inspired by the hydrology of south Florida, where the flow of water seems natural but is in fact highly engineered. The water level in the park is regulated by a system of upstream canals and levees that provide flood control for coastal developments. Water—the lifeblood of the park—enters only after being diverted for other uses. Far from being an unspoiled wilderness, the Everglades is a hybrid landscape, neither natural nor artificial. This ambiguity is reflected in the building, which takes the form of a watery, tree-filled island in the swamp.

The hotel is located in the Shark River Slough just south of the Tamiami Trail, the two-lane highway that is the park's northern border. The Tamiami Trail runs due west from central Miami, passing from the turquoise pools of Miami Beach to the wooden boardwalks and self-guided nature trails of the national park. Both programs find a home in the building, as the hotel expands to include an aquatics center with pools for sport and recreation, as well as a visitors center that interprets the landscape of the slough, with its open marshland dotted with tree islands.

The hotel's formal strategy is adapted from the architecture of the nearby water-pumping stations, which suggest sinking a massive building into the swamp to occupy the most dynamic part of the landscape—the shifting level of the water itself. In the Everglades, subtle changes of even just a few inches in the water level support radically different plant communities. The tree islands of the slough host multiple plant ecosystems (tropical hardwoods, willows, bays, and cypress trees) depending on their elevation, which varies over the area of each island.

These tree-island ecosystems are re-created in the building by manipulating the water level within a series of enclosed courtyards. Taken together, the courtyards form a condensed and accessible version of the park's vast and remote wilderness. The "natural" landscaped courtyards are complemented by the "artificial" pools of the aquatics center, resulting in a landscape of extreme juxtapositions: for instance, an Olympic pool is separated from an alligator hole by just a few feet. Such juxtapositions happen in subtle ways throughout the park, in which narrow levees divide landscapes distinguished by differences in water level.

While the upper level of the building provides the experience of radical difference, the lower level offers an intimate experience with a particular environment. Visitors descend into the hotel rooms, which are located in close proximity to the water.

The rooms are grouped around small lobbies and arranged so that each line of rooms opens onto a different environment, either a landscaped courtyard or an artificial pool. Visitors' awareness of the water level outside is heightened by sectional changes within the room itself, which steps up from the oversize bath to a projecting balcony.

The result is a building that condenses and amplifies existing conditions—programmatic, environmental, tectonic—in the Everglades and south Florida. In concentrating the vast landscape to a self-contained "island," the hotel becomes a microcosm of the park that amplifies and raises awareness of the contradictions inherent in this complex site.

2.A.1
Aerial view of model.

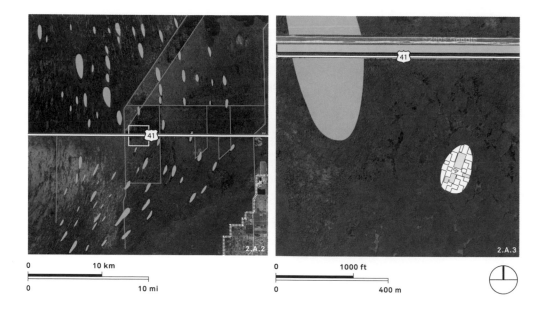

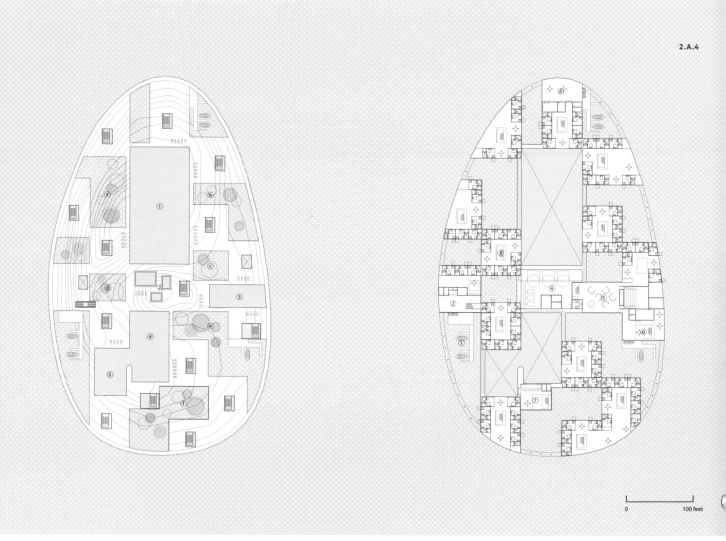

2.A.4

2.A.2
Site diagram.

2.A.3
Enlarged site diagram.

2.A.4
Floor plans.

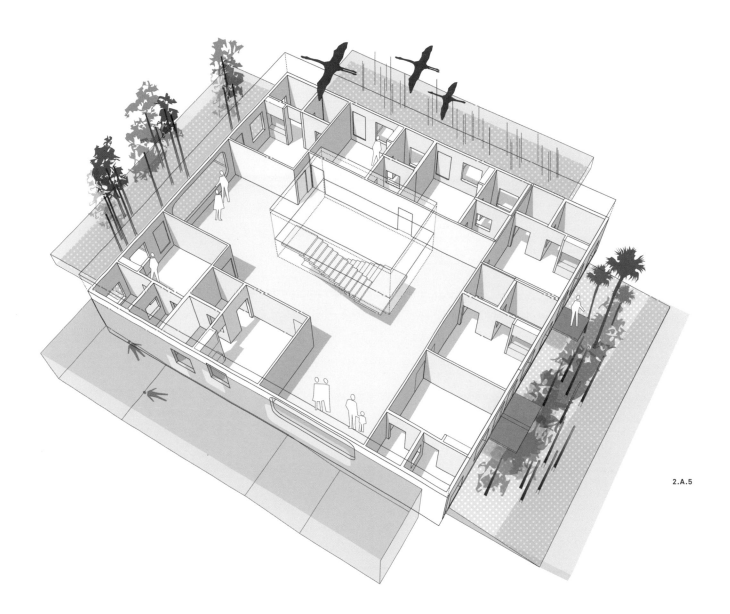

2.A.5

2.A.5
Axonometric of hotel
lobby. Each line of rooms
opens onto a different
aquatic environment.

2.B
Thomas Moran

National park lodges are an unusual opportunity to bring together diverse forms of habitation. Both campsites and hotel rooms create a state of exception particular to travel. Out of one's element, one is open to try new things. These novel behaviors might be as mundane as using the bathroom outdoors or having an extra drink at the bar. Or they could be as out of the ordinary as wrestling an alligator or cheating on one's spouse. This mind-frame influenced by travel contrasts sharply with the didactic quality of national park visitors centers. These centers are designed to not only spatially orient one to the park, but also to instruct the visitor on how to read and interpret nature and its relationship to human civilization. Through dioramas, overlooks, trail maps, and wildlife guides, the visitors-center has become emblematic of a benign but always present government bureaucracy that instructs its citizenry on the correct use of nature. Rather than keep these contrasting programs separate, this project combines and conflates the visitors center and lodge programs. The intention is to undermine the clear nature/culture distinction made by the visitors-center program by letting the domestic practices of the lodge program take on new forms. Influenced by early Team 10 projects analyzing housing typologies, this project assumes leisure programs are an opportunity to experiment with dwelling typologies. The site strategy challenges the conventional low-density, sprawling planning of most national parks. Instead, all the park's program is concentrated in one place, creating a village where park program and dwelling program overlap and interact.

Rather than assigning rooms, the campground strategy of "sites" is deployed. The undulating, stepped building form provides spatial situations one can choose. The landscape is populated with furniture pieces designed to approximate and reconsider conventional domestic activities. One can sleep in a tent and eat at a formal dining table. Or sleep in a well-appointed couchette and cook over a campfire. The goal is to create an experience in which the conventions of habitation are called into question. The park user confronts nature not as something foreign and exotic but as ingrained in the domestic practices of everyday life. Everyday life, accordingly, is challenged and liberated by the presence of wild plants and animals and the state of mind associated with natural settings.

2.B.1
Interior perspective.

2.B.1

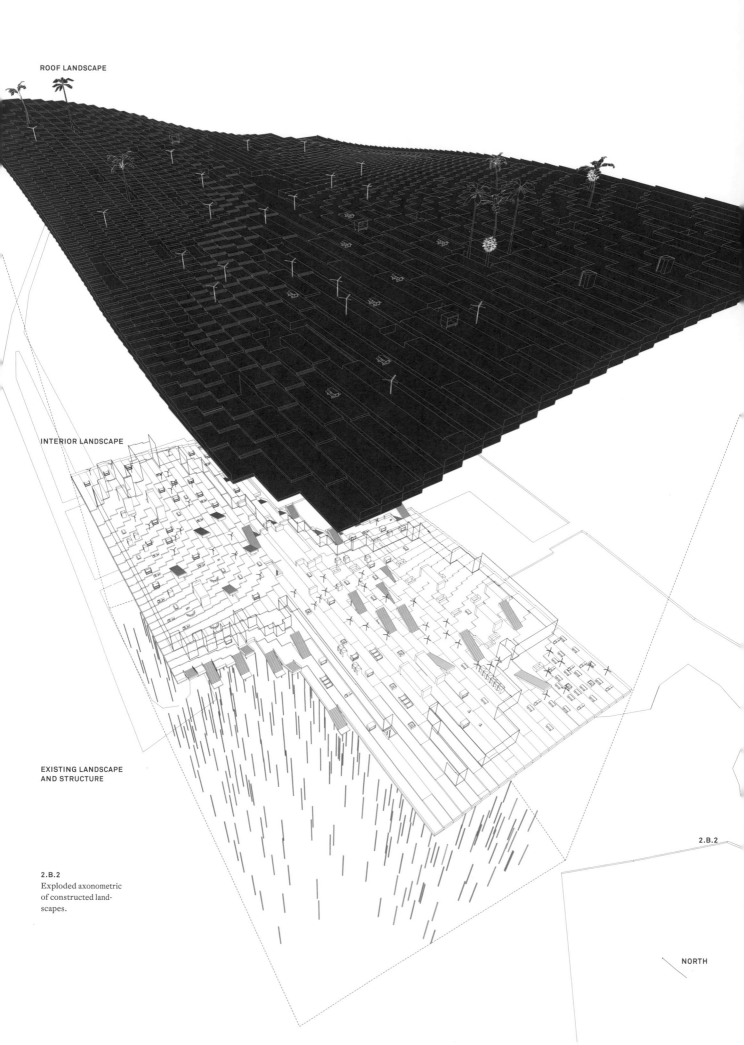

ROOF LANDSCAPE

INTERIOR LANDSCAPE

EXISTING LANDSCAPE
AND STRUCTURE

2.B.2
Exploded axonometric
of constructed land-
scapes.

2.B.2

NORTH

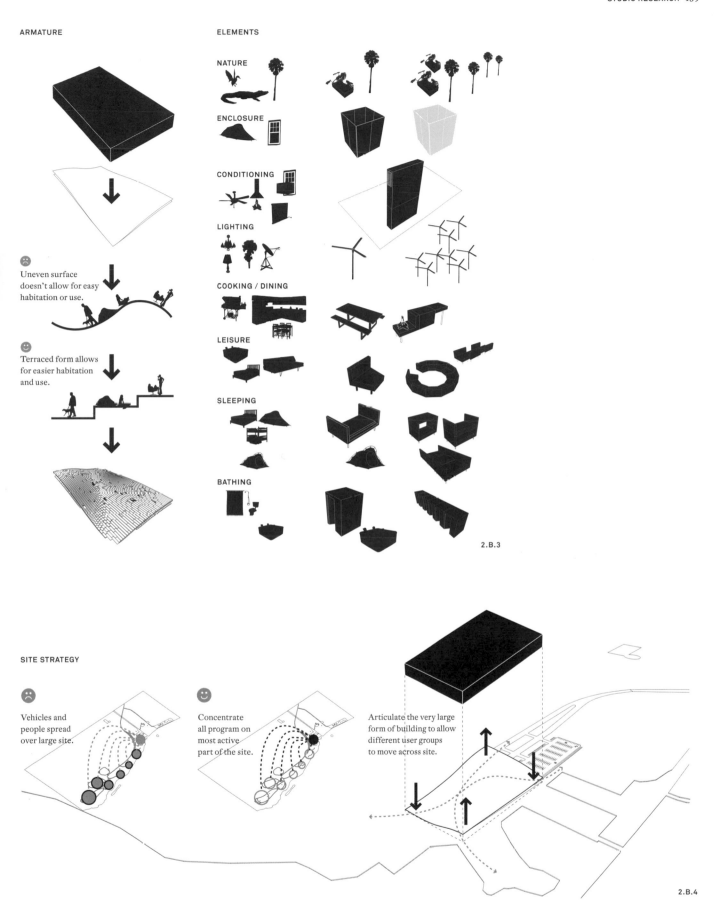

ARMATURE

ELEMENTS

NATURE

ENCLOSURE

CONDITIONING

LIGHTING

COOKING / DINING

LEISURE

SLEEPING

BATHING

Uneven surface doesn't allow for easy habitation or use.

Terraced form allows for easier habitation and use.

2.B.3

SITE STRATEGY

Vehicles and people spread over large site.

Concentrate all program on most active part of the site.

Articulate the very large form of building to allow different user groups to move across site.

2.B.4

2.B.3
Design elements and armatures.

2.B.4
Site strategy diagram.

2.c
Yoo Jung Lee

"Chickee," one of the camping types at the Everglades National Park, served as a project inspiration in the interrogation of the relationship between conflicting desires for access to the wild and the demands of a volatile ecosystem. This small one-room camping unit made of wood is raised on stilts above the water, keeping visitors dry but also providing direct access to the water. This dwelling type has the possibility to represent an amphibious way to live in Everglades National Park.

In the Everglades, nature can be recognized as a combination of two systems: a ground system at the urban scale of the highway coming from Miami and, at the small scale, hiking trails for tours of the Everglades. It can also be seen at two scales: in the water system, which at the large scale is where the waterway meets the Atlantic ocean and provides a connection between the ocean and the park and, at the small scale, where water can be experienced by canoe, kayak, fishing, and water sports.

This project site is the West Lake Trail area in which both the hiking trail and water trail meet. This site provides the chance to think about a place defined by both ground and water characteristics and also about the way these characteristics combine with each other.

The programs in this project consist of three levels: the first is public area; the second is street furniture, which works as both public and private; and the third is a private housing system. Public areas in this project are restaurant (dry area), swimming pool (wet area), and visitors center (dry and wet). There are three kinds of street furniture: wooden plates (dry area), water pond (wet area), and tunnel window (dry and wet). Similarly, private housing is divided into three elements: bedroom (dry area), bathroom (wet area), and living room (dry and wet). The living room can be configured into two, three, or four units, with the street furniture located in the living-room area defined as private or public and generating different activities depending on the different characteristics.

The water level changes seasonally, influencing the shape of the site's boundary; for instance, in the summer, the water level is five feet high, and during the winter it is three feet high. In this way, the project retains an amphibious character.

Between natural and artificial, water and ground, tourism and dwelling, this project challenges us to consider the possibilities an ambiguous place provides, making us ponder ways to live beyond that of the familiar city or town.

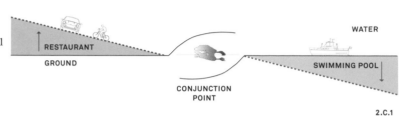

2.C.1

2.C.2

2.C.3

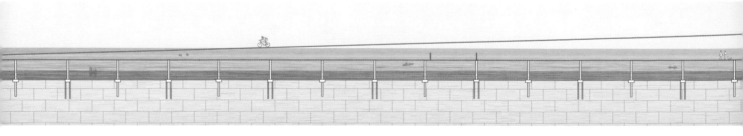

2.C.1
Site strategy.

2.C.2
Perspectival view.

2.C.3
Perspectival view.

2.C.4

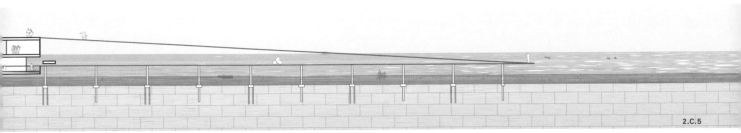

2.C.5

2.C.4
Bird's-eye perspective.

2.C.5
Site section.

3. Datum
The theme, Datum, explores projects in which the architectural proposal acts as a datum against which the natural qualities of the site are registered and amplified. These projects intensify and make explicit the fluctuations within the natural systems.

3.A
Jeff McBride

The Everglades is a very difficult place to appreciate, largely because it is such a muted landscape. From all outward appearances it is monotonous: a wetland with tall grass, water, and trees. It is easy to understand why people for generations have scoffed at the idea this area should be considered a national park.

However, just beneath the surface, this landscape is a teeming ecosystem, home to unique species of a vast array of plants and animals, all held together in an extremely delicate balance. In fact, it is this delicate balance that makes this site so impressive. Everything in the site—plants, animals, fish, and landscape—are tied together so carefully that without everything working in concert, it has the potential to fall like a house of cards. This project developed out of the goal of not only keeping that house of cards standing but also to educate visitors about the wildly diverse and interesting Everglades landscape, thus underlining its need to be preserved.

One of the most ecologically diverse sites in the Everglades is called a tree island. These islands dot the middle of the Everglades and are home to two-thirds of all the plants and animals of the park; broadly scattered, they are largely inaccessible. This eco-hotel is sited on one of these islands, following the path an airboat had already made as part of tourist excursions. Over time, this airboat gash would heal and the tree island would grow around the new eco-hotel.

The cross section of any tree island is composed of numerous different landscapes packed very tightly together, each unique and with its own features and interests. For the eco-hotel, communal programmatic elements are placed along the path at elevations that maximize views of what makes that specific area unique. For instance, at the entrance of the hotel are the sawgrass glades, where the diverse flora and fauna at the water level is made visible by lowering the building at this point. A short distance beyond are the Cypress Heads, where the bromelians and birds are strikingly beautiful, so the public spaces are placed higher to allow visitors the best view of the landscape. The building is a sectional response to the landscape.

In order to protect the delicate environment, the building is constructed out of large plates of steel for its intensive structural potentials and its potentially productive materiality in the remediation of the natural species. The park is in danger of being destroyed by agricultural development, which is dumping high concentrations of nutrients, specifically phosphorus, into the park's water supply and allowing invasive species to take over (according to some estimates, cattail, an invasive species, is taking over the park at a rate of two acres a day). One solution to this problem is to chemically remove the phosphorus from the water supply, thereby making the water ideal for the nutrient-deprived vegetation. The filtering process involves a small chemical reaction in which iron combines with phosphorus to produce iron phosphate, a benign, nonsoluble product. The most beneficial design, then, would maximize the amount of iron in the water supply for the greatest beneficial effect on the landscape. Thus, the building was constructed of exposed, rusting steel panels. Over time, the rusting steel will flake off, removing phosphorus and protecting the plants downstream.

Steel-plate construction makes construction easier by reducing the overall interference on the island. Structural modeling was done to confirm that this steel-plate construction needs to only contact the ground at two locations and can span five hundred feet between each point of support. The building essentially becomes a bridge, reducing the amount of ground contact and allowing for most of the construction to take place above the water level.

There is little precedent for designing in a place like the Everglades; the climate, the landscape, and the ecology are highly unusual. The new eco-hotel, while an inevitable intrusion into this site, is meant to have a harmonious impact by occupying a previously disturbed site, reducing the building footprint, and chemically removing the high nutrient levels in the water. As a result, the new eco-hotel would not only positively market the Everglades to the outside world, but it would also expose visitors to the diverse and almost completely unseen landscape inside the tree islands.

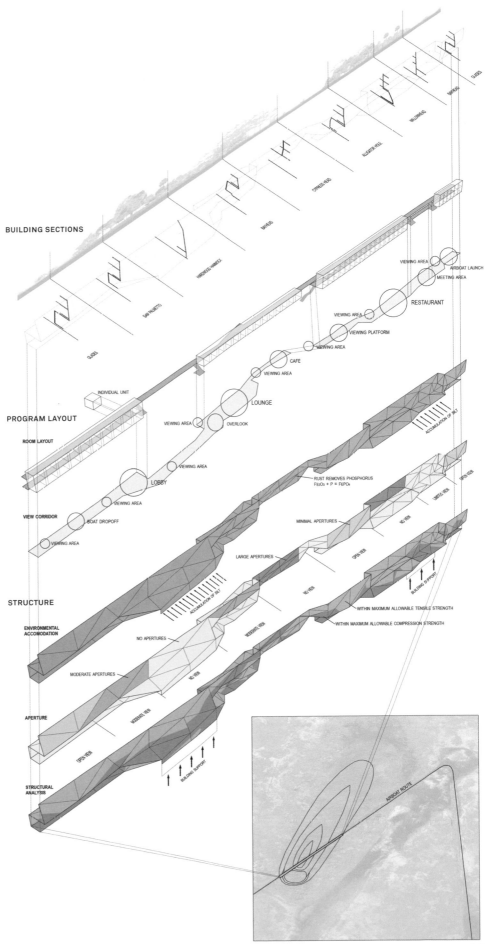

BUILDING SECTIONS

GLADES

SAW PALMETTO

HARDWOOD HAMMOCK

BAYHEAD

CYPRESS HEAD

ALLIGATOR HOLE

WILLOWHEAD

GLADES

PROGRAM LAYOUT

INDIVIDUAL UNIT

VIEWING AREA

AIRBOAT LAUNCH

MEETING AREA

RESTAURANT

VIEWING AREA

VIEWING PLATFORM

VIEWING AREA

CAFE

VIEWING AREA

LOUNGE

ROOM LAYOUT

VIEWING AREA

OVERLOOK

VIEWING AREA

LOBBY

VIEWING AREA

VIEW CORRIDOR

BOAT DROPOFF

VIEWING AREA

STRUCTURE

ACCUMULATION OF SILT

RUST REMOVES PHOSPHORUS
$Fe_2O_3 + P = FePO_4$

MINIMAL APERTURES

OPEN VIEW

LIMITED VIEW

ENVIRONMENTAL
ACCOMODATION

ACCUMULATION OF SILT

LARGE APERTURES

NO VIEW

BUILDING SUPPORT

WITHIN MAXIMUM ALLOWABLE TENSILE STRENGTH

NO APERTURES

MODERATE VIEW

WITHIN MAXIMUM ALLOWABLE COMPRESSION STRENGTH

MODERATE APERTURES

NO VIEW

APERTURE

MODERATE VIEW

OPEN VIEW

STRUCTURAL
ANALYSIS

BUILDING SUPPORT

AIRBOAT ROUTE

3.A.1
Exploding axonometric
of lodge elements.

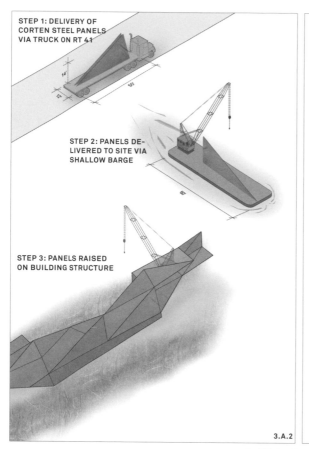

STEP 1: DELIVERY OF
CORTEN STEEL PANELS
VIA TRUCK ON RT 41

STEP 2: PANELS DE-
LIVERED TO SITE VIA
SHALLOW BARGE

STEP 3: PANELS RAISED
ON BUILDING STRUCTURE

3.A.2

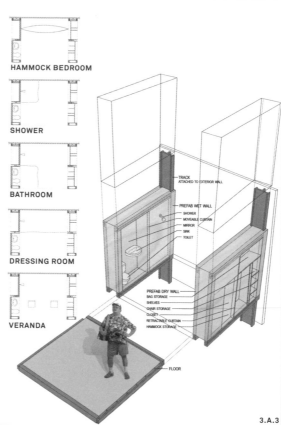

HAMMOCK BEDROOM

SHOWER

BATHROOM

DRESSING ROOM

VERANDA

TRACK
ATTACHED TO EXTERIOR WALL

PREFAB WET WALL
SHOWER
MOVEABLE CURTAIN
MIRROR
SINK
TOILET

PREFAB DRY WALL
BAG STORAGE
SHELVES
CHAIR STORAGE
CLOSET
RETRACTABLE CURTAIN
HAMMOCK STORAGE

FLOOR

3.A.3

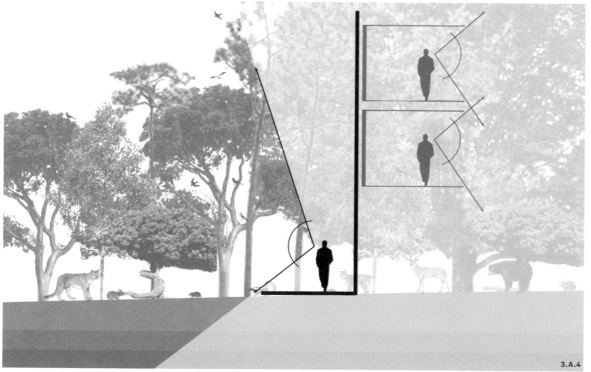

3.A.4

3.A.2
Synthesis of building-
material delivery and
construction. Steel
building material was
selected because of its
iron content's ability
to filter phosphorus
pollutants from water
systems.

3.A.3
Room plans and
diagram.

3.A.4
Schematic section
and view angles into
surrounding habitat.

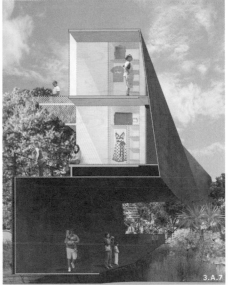

3.A.5
Sectional perspective
through eco-hotel.

3.A.6
Sectional perspective.

3.A.7
Sectional perspective
through rooms.

3.A.8
Site model showing
building datum.

3.B
Brook Denison

This project, "Tree Island," delights in the play between natural and artificial, exploring the complicated relationship between a program fit for a Miami Beach resort that happens to be situated within a national park. Historically, the Florida Everglades has been misunderstood and mistreated; often thought of as a swamp, most early efforts sought to conquer the land by draining it. Only recently has it been recognized for what it is: a singular system of vast, slow-moving, spring-fed freshwater rivers stemming from the middle of the state, covering millions of acres with shallow, clean water. The eco-system harbors animals and plants specific to the wetland, along with growing throngs of invasive species who live together under constant threat of invasion and contamination from south Florida's booming population.

The National Parks Service is more than a land conservancy; in reality, its mission is equally dedicated to preserving these environments as it is to providing the public with sustainable options for exploring them. Unlike a wilderness preserve, many national parks include lodging and dining in addition to networks of trails, which are supplemented by guides coupled with jeeps, boats, vans, and other conveyance.

Thus, the Florida Everglades National Park can be thought of as a preservation and conservation effort composed of engineered responses to scientific research and data. Equally important, though, is the public education campaign, which is anchored in providing an Everglades experience to the mildly adventurous taxpayer. Accordingly, the hotels, air-boats, lodges, trails, rangers, and guided trolley visits are just as important as the seven-billion-dollar investment the federal government has made in pursuit of a vast network of levees, bridges, canals, floodgates, monitoring stations, reservoirs, and personnel to stabilize this singular habitat. It is by no means a simple system. The Everglades is a negotiation among politicians, scientists, tourists, local communities, sugar companies, alligator farmers, and hospitality staff—just to name some of the groups with a stake in the Everglades.

This Everglades resort project is situated on an island intersected by an abandoned levee. The site selected juxtaposes the straight, artificial line of the levee against the natural, amorphous mound of the island, situating the building in a spot with allegiances to both the natural and the artificial. The straight bar of lodging rooms mimics the linearity of the levee by arranging the rooms in a continuous line while gradually lifting above the treetops to a heightened remove. The lodger's perspective is ideal for viewing the sublimely flat Florida landscape—an idea borrowed from a nearby 1960s-era concrete viewing platform that spirally ascends more than 150 feet to an unforgettable view of the vast wetland. Rising away from the hotel's public facilities, the lodging rooms strive to provide guests with a meditative remove, abstracting the Everglades landscape into patterns and textures which are occasionally intersected by the straight line of a highway, levee, or canal.

To accommodate other public facilities—such as a restaurant, pool, bar, and nightclub—the linear form drops down to the ground and coils around itself, creating a suitable enclosure for the public amenities while transforming the rigid linearity of artificial forms into an amorphous, "naturally" shaped public area. The play between the two—straight and curved, artificial and natural—suggests an interdependence paralleling the artificially constructed natural environment of the Everglades.

The National Parks Service strives to strike a delicate balance between nature and tourism. Rather than protecting land by exclusion, it safely exposes to the public an area that subtly advocates the program's worthiness while offering a sanctioned tour through otherwise protected land. Following the national parks model, this project proposes a resort in the middle of the Everglades that exposes the natural and scenic beauty of the environment to a vacationing population. This is not, strictly speaking, environmental preservation. Rather, it is a mix of responsible land use and outdoor exploration, coupled with resort amenities typically found in Miami Beach. The majority of the proposed building perches atop thin stilts to minimize its impact on the ground. While the architectural response is calibrated to the environment's stability, it is also tuned to maximize the visitors' experience with Everglades National Park.

Descending from the monastic rooms above the trees, visitors socialize in the resort pool and bar, where the meditative Everglades scenery is transformed into a thematic backdrop that can be viewed through openings in stark white surfaces, reminiscent of the South Beach resorts of a bygone era. These spaces nestle inward, offering protection from the creatures of the wilderness beyond as well as distance from the granola and National Parks Service green-on-yellow aesthetics typically associated with national parks. In these interiorized environments, the landscape is viewed as a trendy texture that shifts color and appearance according to the season, augmenting the bar and pool with a backdrop that vaguely recalls the environment but is much more focused on cocktails.

3.B.1
Sectional perspective
of pool.

3.B.2
Interior perspective
rendering of single
hotel room.

3.B.3
Side elevation.

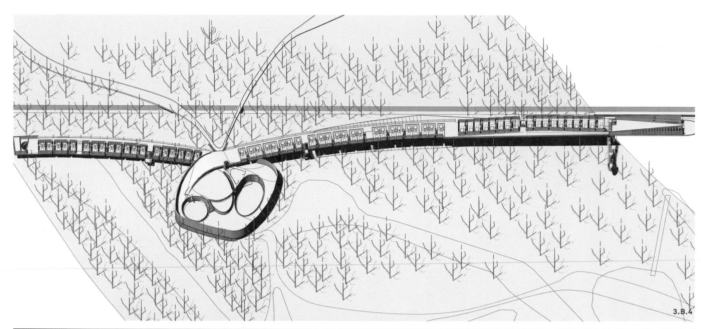

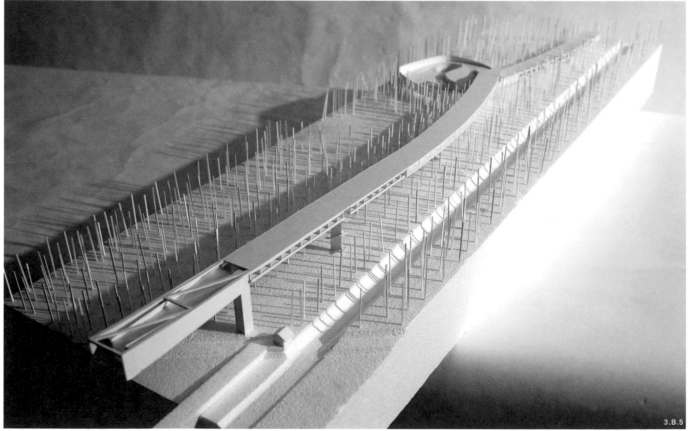

3.B.4
Overall site model.

3.B.5
Model image.

3.C
Heather Loeffler

This lodge is designed to question the appropriateness of normative hotel dwelling and view configurations for guest rooms in a national park marked by the constant presence of water and endless horizontal vistas. It proposes that a visit to a national park should be accompanied by a style of dwelling that moves away from the repetitive, the daily, and the mundane. The lodge relies on water, luminosity, volume, and structure to create an experience that maintains an intimate relationship with the site.

The program for the proposed replacement lodge at Everglades National Park is spread throughout three permeable layers: a floating-dock level for visitors arriving or departing by boat or who want to relax at the edge of the semi-liquid park; the lobby/guest room/dining and information-services level, accessed by land for those arriving by car or from the dock below; and the wet, cooling roof deck, accessed from the dock or from room level. A series of *compluvium* and *impluvium* allows light, air, and water to permeate the building, playing a prominent role in the project. Throughout the lodge, these two elements provide for rainwater collection and redistribution as well as visual connections to nature, reminding visitors of the prominent and ever-present element of the park: water.

The lodge contains two types of rooms for guests and a third type of room for full-time or part-time staff. The larger guest rooms offer views of the sky via ventilating solar tubes (these tubes also prevent against heat transfer) and of the sea below via in-ground double-hammock openings. The smaller guest rooms provide views through the pool, which acts as a clerestory window allowing diffused light into the rooms and down to the sea via single in-ground hammock openings. The hammocks hovering over the sea in both guest-room types and the skylight shafts offer a means of natural ventilation and direct visceral and visual connections to the "wild" nature preserve, creating an experience suggestive of camping while indoors. This non-normative view configuration of sky and sea acts in direct opposition to the endless lateral views offered throughout the park.

Designed to sit on a series of lally columns over the sea, the lodge siting breaks from the familiar hotel experience, producing new connections to the sea while allowing for extreme habitation and a rethinking of commonplace notions of stability, ground, and enclosure. As the compluvium, the cistern, and the hammock openings act as an integrated drainage system, the three permeable layers permit both rainwater and, in extreme conditions, flood water to flow through the building. The collection of lally columns that allow the building to sit at the shoreline and act as conduit for plumbing and electrical wiring also produce an overnight experience above the water.

The organization of the plan is based on duration of visit, mode of arrival, and guest services desired. The plan divides the program into land and sea areas. The visitors center and restaurant are located adjacent to the parking lot at the land side of the building, allowing tourists to make a quick stop for information or a snack (without walking through the lodge) before heading back to the park entrance. This context also provides overnight guests with privacy and keeps the noisier elements of the program—cars, groups, bar, dining—separate from the guest rooms. The building meets the land with a large ramp that acts as an outdoor classroom—an extension of the building—for gathering larger tour groups before an outing. The ramp also allows for the convenient delivery of goods to an otherwise difficult location for deliveries. The "wet area" roof deck spans the lodge, acting as the connection between land, sea, day visitors, overnight guests, the reality of the park, and the luxury of a vacation. All other aspects of the program are located above the water, including a lap pool, a large communal open-air hammock, and all guest and staff rooms, reinforcing the lodge's centrality and role within the park.

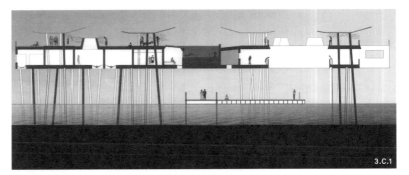

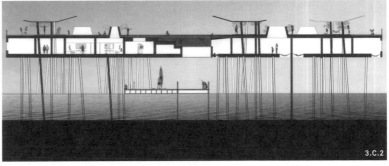

3.C.1
Building cross-section.

3.C.2
Building cross-section.

3.C.3
Building cross-section.

3.C.4
Perspective view
into wet area.

3.C.5
Interior perspective.

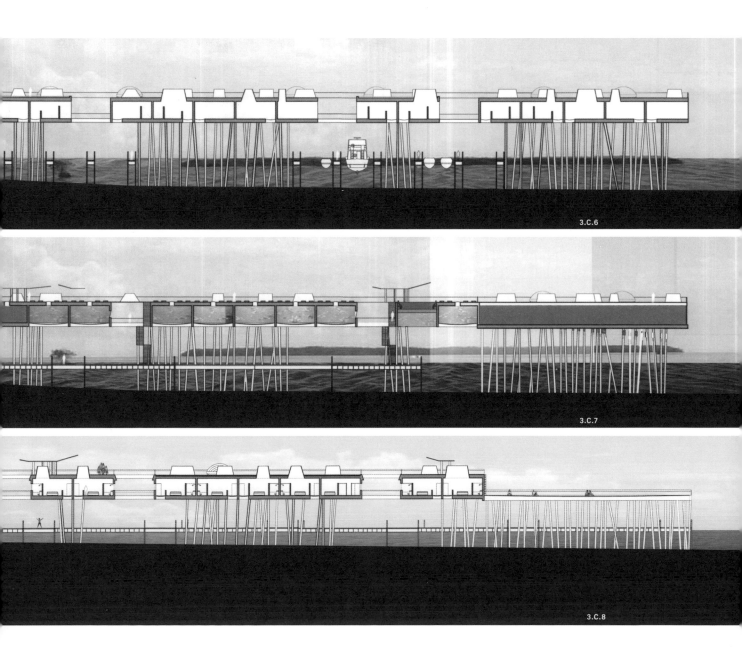

3.C.6
Building cross-section.

3.C.7
Building cross-section.

3.C.8
Longitudinal section.

IMAGE CREDITS